OPPORTUNITIES IN
FOREIGN LANGUAGE CAREERS

Theodore Huebener

VGM Career Horizons
A Division of National Textbook Company
4255 West Touhy Avenue
Lincolnwood, Illinois 60646-1975

Photo Credits

Front Cover: upper left, United Nations/
M. Grant; upper right, Department of
Communications, Research Center, Ottawa,
Ontario, Canada, Crown Copyright Photo;
lower left, University of Illinois, at Chicago
Circle; lower right, United Airlines.
Back cover: upper left, NTC; upper right, United
Nations/M. Tsovaras; lower left, NTC; lower
right, United Nations.

1985 Printing

ABOUT THE AUTHOR

Theodore Huebener is Supervisor of Student Teachers of Foreign Language at New York University. For twenty-five years he was the Director of Foreign Languages in the schools of the city of New York, the largest single language department in the United States. A native New Yorker, he received degrees from the College of the City of New York (A.B.) and from Columbia University (M.A.). He did his graduate work at Yale University where he secured the Ph.D. degree in 1932.

He began his professional career as an elementary teacher in the New York school system. In rapid succession he became high school teacher, head of a high school department of foreign languages, summer high school principal, assistant director of foreign languages, and finally director of foreign languages.

Dr. Huebener has given courses at the City College, Hunter College, New York University, and Fairleigh Dickinson University. He is a frequent contributor to professional journals here and abroad and is the author and coauthor of 53 textbooks in five languages which are used throughout the United States and Canada. As an authority in the field of foreign language methodology, he has served on many local and national committees.

Dr. Huebener's training has been largely academic, but in his youth he also learned bookkeeping, typewriting, stenography, and Spanish commercial correspondence. For several years he worked for a number of firms, including an import house, General Motors, the American Sugar Refining Company, and Huyler's. Thus, he has had firsthand contacts with the business world, adding to his qualifications for the writing of this manual.

At various times, Dr. Huebener has been the guest of the foreign offices of France, West Germany, Israel, and Italy. In 1950 and 1951, he served as Consultant in Education for the State Department in its HICOG program in West Germany. As a member of the Overseas Speakers Bureau of the United States Information Agency, Dr. Huebener has lectured almost every summer in various countries of Europe and Africa.

TABLE OF CONTENTS

Historical background. Foreign languages in the United States. Bilingual Education. Importance of foreign languages. Need for trained personnel. Jobs as reflected in want-ads. Comments of business and professional people. Language in business. Returns to be expected. Attributes necessary for success.

High School. College. The Choice of a foreign language. The decision is yours. Getting practice. Special training. Preparation for a bilingual office job. Planning your courses. Preparation for government service. Preparation for international careers.

Help Wanted. Writing the letter of application. Personal interview. Employment agencies. Employment abroad. Positions wanted. Securing a job in South America. Business openings. Government positions. Analysis of the job. Types of positions. Your duties on the job.

CHAPTER 1

THE FIELD OF FOREIGN LANGUAGES

Because of the dominant position of the United States in world affairs, there is at present, and there will continue to be in the foreseeable future, a demand for large numbers of men and women who are in command of a foreign language. In fact, the field is so wide that there is room not only for the expert with near-native competency in several languages but also for the person who has but a bowing acquaintance with one foreign tongue. However great or meager one's knowledge of a foreign language may be, it is a cultural and a vocational asset.

There is a wide range of jobs open to linguists, extending all the way from that of the bilingual stenographer or clerk to the highly skilled interpreter at the U.N. Positions are available in the business world, teaching, and government service.

In the business world, export trade, international advertising, and engineering construction in foreign countries are the areas where knowledge of a language is especially useful. However, it should be stated right at the start that language is but an additional asset; in most cases, the job depends on technical or professional skill or knowledge.

In government, available positions are chiefly in the foreign service. On the whole, they are interesting and remunerative and, in addition, provide opportunities for travel. The State Department employs many civilians abroad, numbering about 5,600,

1

and because of the role of the U.S. in world affairs, the need for a large staff abroad undoubtedly will continue.

Despite the drop in the number of students enrolling in four-year colleges, the study of foreign languages is still an important major. In addition, the demand in business for personnel with language competence has caused a considerable increase in the enrollments of private language schools.

A new movement in foreign languages, which has the strong support of the federal government and is supported by millions of dollars in national funds, is bilingual education. The program, which is spreading rapidly, offers many jobs in a variety of foreign languages on all school levels.

HISTORICAL BACKGROUND

During the Middle Ages, Latin was the universal language of the cultured, at least as far as Western Europe was concerned. It was the official language of the church and universities. Lectures, disquisitions, and discussions were conducted in that tongue. All state documents and scientific treatises were written in Latin. The first printed book, the Gutenberg Bible, appeared in Latin. Since this language was indispensable for any higher education, it was the mainstay of school instruction, especially on the secondary level.

From the time of the disintegration of the Roman Empire, however, the popular Latin spoken in the marketplace and in military camps gradually assumed new aspects. Endings were dropped, case forms were simplified, and pronunciation was changed. In the former provinces of the Empire, new national languages developed—French, Spanish, Italian, Portuguese, and Roumanian—the so-called "Romance" languages. Since only the Rhine had been occupied by the Romans, the language of Germany was not deeply affected by Latin. In Great Britain,

English developed out of the Anglo-Saxon of the Germanic invaders, the Latin of the church, and the French of the Norman conquerors in the eleventh century.

These national languages continued to develop and to assert themselves. During the Renaissance, such distinguished writers as Dante and Petrarch began to use the vernacular for prose and poetry. Latin gradually was dropped as a medium of literary expression. The wider employment of the vernacular as a medium of instruction in the schools received great impetus from the Reformation, which stressed the reading of the Bible by the common man.

Slowly but surely everyday speech also invaded the universities and other seats of learning. As early as the beginning of the sixteenth century, Paracelsus, the noted physician and philosopher, attacked the use of Latin and the barren learning of the scholars and proceeded to give his lectures in German. In France, the famous essayist, Montaigne records that in 1539, at the age of six, he was sent to the distinguished college of Guyenne, where the tongue of the Romans was no longer spoken.

It was not, however, until the middle of the eighteenth century that Latin was displaced as the standard medium of communication in higher institutions of learning. A leader in bringing this about was the philosopher and mathematician Leibniz, who stressed the importance of modern languages.

Succeeding the classical languages of Latin and Greek in the curriculum of the secondary schools and partly displacing them, the modern languages took over, in large part, the traditional grammar method employed in teaching the ancient tongues. Like the latter, they became essentially school subjects, taught for their educational and cultural values as an introduction to literary studies.

Intelligent people realized very soon that dealing with a living tongue in this manner was ineffective. One of the most significant comments is that of the Moravian educator Comenius who says in his *Magna Didacta* (1632): "Every language must be learned by practice rather than by rules, especially by reading, repeating, copying, and by written and oral attempts at imitation."

This important basic principle, however, was ignored. It was not until the nineteenth century, with the rise of psychology and experimentation in the learning processes, that language experts developed more effective methods of acquiring a foreign tongue. James Hamilton stressed the need of introducing the student to the living language from the beginning. Other reformers developed a so-called "natural" method. Among these was a German, Gottlieb Heness, and a Frenchman, Sauveur, who started a private language school in 1866 in New Haven. Out of their fruitful endeavors grew the summer language school with its short, intensive courses.

Claude Marcel, who published a significant treatise on language teaching in 1867, stood for the dictum: "Learn to read by reading." He exerted considerable influence on language teaching, especially in the United States.

In the New World, there was a great interest in various foreign languages from the earliest times. New England, particularly, was favored with persons of a scholarly bent, and the libraries of clergymen, doctors, and lawyers frequently contained books in French, German, Italian, Spanish, and Latin. Many of the more educated people took private lessons from native tutors.

Benjamin Franklin was an ardent student of foreign languages and did much to promote their instruction. In his *Autobiography,* he tells how he progressed in his linguistic pursuits: "I had begun in 1733 to study languages; I soon made myself so much a Master of the French as to be able to read the books with ease. I then undertook the Italian." Practical-minded as he was, he recommended Latin, Greek, and French for students of medicine; Latin and French for law students; and French, German, and Spanish for those entering the business world. At the National Academy of Sciences, which Franklin helped to found, the first teacher of French, German, Italian, and music was a German.

GERMAN

During the nineteenth century, German was taught extensively in many private and public schools, and throughout the United States, many day schools were founded by German-Americans who wanted the language transmitted to their children. The extent and influence of these German schools was amazing. They became so numerous that a school law enacted in Pennsylvania placed them on a par with the English schools. In Ohio, the 1840 legislature directed all boards of education to introduce German wherever it was requested by seven citizens.

In the early 1900s, German was taught in the elementary schools of St. Louis, Baltimore, Cleveland, Chicago, Dayton, Denver, Buffalo, Milwaukee, St. Paul, San Francisco, and New York. As late as 1914, one-third of the entire elementary school population of Cincinnati was learning German.

German enjoyed this favorable position until the entry of the United States into World War I. At that time, enrollments dropped drastically, and only a little more than one-half of one percent of the total high school population was enrolled in German. After the war, however, the language experienced a rapid recovery and returned to its former popularity.

FRENCH

French has always been regarded as a "prestige" language, particularly after its appearance in the curriculum of the Boston Latin School in 1852. The number of persons in the United States who speak French as a native language is very small when compared to native Germans and Italians; however, this fact has not adversely affected the popularity of the language. Despite a drop in the number of French immigrants to the United States in recent years, the language has maintained its cultural prestige and its place in the American school curriculum.

ITALIAN

Although millions of Italians have come to the United States, that language has never maintained very strong enrollments. Although Italian was offered at colleges and universities, it did not enter public school curriculums until 1922, when it was placed on a par with other languages in New York City.

SPANISH

Spanish, like Italian, historically had many ardent devotees. During the nineteenth century, however, it seldom appeared in the curricula of schools and colleges. Only in some elementary schools of New Mexico was it a subject of instruction. The War with Mexico (1846-1848) stimulated a short-lived interest in the language, however, the greatest boon to Spanish came with the outbreak of World War I. Enrollments rose from 36,000 in 1915 to 252,000 in 1922. One of the great public incentives to study Spanish was the popular notion that increased trade with Latin America would provide many new and lucrative positions for young Americans. The large influx of Puerto Ricans and Cubans into the United States in the last few decades also has given a strong boost to Spanish enrollments. In recent years, Spanish has almost doubled in the high schools, rising from a little over one million students in 1960 to nearly two million in later years. Spanish now occupies first place in enrollment figures among modern languages.

FOREIGN LANGUAGES IN THE UNITED STATES

The interest in foreign languages and their study in schools and colleges has fluctuated widely over the years, reflecting emotional reactions to economic situations and international relations. For decades, the study of foreign languages was slighted in the United States because, unlike Europe, there was no economic or social pressure to learn a foreign language. In American schools, study of a second language has always been on an elective basis, whereas in Europe, it is a required subject which is considered to be of great importance. Americans tended to ignore the value of a foreign language for communication and intelligence service and, as we have mentioned, German almost disappeared from the curriculums of most schools because of emotions aroused by World War I. By the time World War II erupted, this lack of foresight had been corrected. It was realized that the knowledge of the enemy's language was a highly useful and necessary weapon. But to the consternation of the military, it was found that our young soldiers were very poorly equipped with even the regularly studied languages. As for a language like Japanese—a knowledge of which was almost urgent—it was discovered that of 200,000 enlisted men and officers in the Navy, just about 15 possessed a workable ability in that language.

Because of the extreme urgency, the Army Specialized Training Program (ASTP) was set up to provide immediate instruction in some 50 foreign languages. Because of intensive teaching methods, many contact hours, selected students, high motivation, the use of phonograph records and films, native "informants," and a singleness of aim (everyday, practical soldier talk), the ASTP achieved marvelous results within a very short time.

The launching of Sputnik by the Russians in 1957 made a startling impact on the Western world. Statesmen, scientists, and educators were shocked into activity. Specialists looked into Russian science and made a study of the educational system of the Soviets, and it was felt in many quarters that their teaching of science and mathematics was superior to ours. Federal authorities realized that training in the areas of science, mathematics, and foreign languages was not merely a matter of vocational preparation, but also a vital function of national defense.

In view of this, the National Defense Education Act (NDEA), which allotted millions of dollars for the training of students, was passed to provide for stronger teaching of science, mathematics, and foreign languages.

Under the NDEA Act, thousands of teachers were trained in summer institutes at the larger colleges and universities. In these programs, linguists conducted research and developed new materials and methods, including one known as the "audio-lingual" approach. Since modern language usage stresses hearing and speaking in this teaching method, widespread use was made of the latest orthophonic devices. The most elaborate of these is, of course, the language laboratory. Today foreign language departments of most reputable schools or colleges use this device.

The NDEA program is still in operation, although only in a very limited way. Federal support has been reduced so much that the institutes for teachers have been dropped. There are still numbers of language "centers" on 50 to 60 campuses, devoted largely to research, area studies, and graduate training. The emphasis in these is on exotic languages.

Within the last few years there has been an enrollment increase in Chinese, Japanese, and Arabic. However, because allotments to support the teaching of these languages have been reduced and the dollar value has declined, it is likely that their study will not show growth in the immediate future.

BILINGUAL EDUCATION

Although the last few years have brought a decline in the enrollments of foreign language classes, a new educational trend which has recently appeared is gathering momentum and gives promise of providing jobs for thousands of foreign language teachers. This new concept is bilingual education, which was originally developed as a plan to give Puerto Rican students basic instruction in the Spanish language. From its original parameters, the idea has developed into an extensive program involving every language spoken by an ethnic group in the United States. Federal and state governments have established agencies and appropriated funds to set up and conduct the program.

All of the larger universities and many colleges now have departments of bilingual education, and many classes have been organized to train teachers on the secondary and elementary school levels. At the present time, it appears that bilingual education will continue to grow and provide jobs for thousands of teachers.

The United States generally is regarded as one of the Anglo-Saxon countries, although large numbers of its people are of other ethnic groups and speak languages other than English. In little over a century more than 42 million immigrants have come to our shores. According to the 1970 census, there were over 9½ million foreign-born persons residing in the United States whose mother tongues were as follows:

French	2,188,000
German	4,892,000
Italian	3,118,000
Polish	2,018,000
Spanish	6,127,000
Yiddish	1,156,000
Other	5,851,000
Not reported	9,222,000

From the above it is evident that the languages most widely spoken in the United States are Spanish, German, and Italian. There are, however, many other languages spoken in various parts of the United States, especially in metropolitan areas. In New York City, for example, there are large numbers of speakers of Chinese, Japanese, Portuguese, Greek, Creole, Lithuanian, Danish, Swedish, Norwegian, and Albanian. In an effort to reach these minorities, special area studies have been undertaken. The Board of Education of New York City is scheduling examinations in some of these languages for elementary school teachers. Millions of dollars are being allotted by the federal government for this program, which is expanding and which will definitely provide jobs for thousands of teachers of foreign languages.

IMPORTANCE OF FOREIGN LANGUAGES

At the end of World War II, the United States emerged as the richest and most powerful nation on earth. From a geographically and culturally isolated nation, America has assumed worldwide obligations, and her troops now are stationed in some 30 nations; her bases stretch from Brazil to Bikini; and her commercial interests encompass the world. Fords run along the mountain roads of Greece; American cigarettes are smoked from Reykjavik to Rangoon; and Coca Cola can be obtained in the most remote hamlets.

That the center of gravity, politically, economically, and culturally, has swung to the United States requires no proof. It is highly significant that the body of international representatives working to establish peace and security, the United Nations, has its headquarters in America. At present, there are thousands of Americans stationed abroad, and it is obvious that more and more will be called upon to serve their government in the years to come. To meet these worldwide obligations and to maintain its cultural leadership, America must provide more effective training for its youth, particularly in foreign languages.

NEED FOR TRAINED PERSONNEL

It is obvious, then, that because of the dominant position of the United States in world affairs, there is at present and there will be in the future an urgent demand for men and women who are in command of a foreign language. The need is apparent in four major areas:

• International business, including the export trade and "overseas" operations of large corporations.

• A great variety of jobs in domestic business, professional callings, and organizations.

• A number of branches of the federal government especially its overseas activities, civilian and military.

• Teaching a foreign language in elementary, secondary schools or college in the United States or abroad in an American or a foreign institution.

Students of international business management work with instructor on their Chinese conversational style.

Photo: American Graduate School of International Management.

JOBS AS REFLECTED IN THE WANT-ADS

In perusing the want-ads of the New York Times, it is evident that there are over 200 positions advertised every Sunday that require competence in a foreign language. During the several weeks from November 1979 to January 1980 there were 3086 ads for foreign language jobs. The totals for the three leading languages were: French 989, German 964, Spanish 967. A lesser number of ads asked for Italian, Portuguese, Russian, Japanese, Chinese, and Hebrew.

The level of competence required in different jobs varies greatly. Sometimes it is quite moderate, as when for instance an ad reads: "Spanish would be useful" or "Knowledge of French helpful." On the other hand, there are many positions in which a higher degree of competence is required. The ad will then use specific terms such as: "Good knowledge; speak-fluent; speak-write; speak-read; read-write; translation; dictation; or bilingual."

There is a wide range of occupations in which a foreign language if not absolutely essential can still be very useful.

The Louisiana State Department of Education compiled the following list.

Airline stewardess/steward	Foreign exchange clerk
Bilingual secretary	Hotel manager
Book dealer	Immigration inspector
Buyer	Importer
Civil Service worker	Intelligence officer
Commercial attaché	International business
Consul	Interpreter
Customs inspector	Journalist
Diplomat	Lawyer
Exporter	Librarian

Philanthropic foundations
Physician
Radio announcer
Radio monitor
Religious organizations
Receptionist
Red Cross
Researcher
Salesman
Social worker

Trade magazine publisher
Translator
Teacher exchange programs
Travel bureau
United Nations
U.S. Government:
    Armed Services
    Foreign Service
    U.S. Information Agency

As is evident from the above list, the range is great. It goes all the way from the office boy who did not complete high school, but who speaks a foreign language, to the executive director of a huge corporation with offices in two dozen countries. Most of the positions, however, are clerical or secretarial, with salaries ranging from $150 to $250 per week.

Here are some typical want-ads for persons with some knowledge of a foreign language:

> SPANISH/Engl Secy   f/pd $250-300
> Park Ave. co. Asst in translating Span
> into Engl & vice/versa. Asst VP.

> GERMAN/ENGLISH   Fee Pd
>   Sec'y to Bank Executive
> $18 - $20,000
> Steno – Both – Stable Work bkgd reqd.

> FRENCH-ENGLISH   Admin Assist $21,000
> Large prestige int'l corp for Sr
> VP. Must have poise, tact & be able
> to deal with hi level mgmt.

Bilingual CUSTOMER SERVICE
Spanish/English, type 40wpm, general
office work. Permanent opportunity.

FRENCH SECY.   to $22,000
Exec.Secy to President of new European
subsidiary.

CRUISE LINE/GERMAN $18,200
Exec VP of large int'l corp needs
secy with gd skills and admin
abilities.

RUSSIAN TRANSLATORS. Engineers only.
Experienced in translating technical
specifications into Russian. Full
time, permanent.

It is evident, then, that there are many interesting positions waiting for qualified persons with foreign language training combined with a technical skill. Usually, knowledge of a foreign language alone will not secure the job, but it is an important and, in some cases, an essential asset.

COMMENTS OF BUSINESS AND PROFESSIONAL PEOPLE

Dr. John H. Furbay, former Director of Air World Education, Kansas City, Missouri, says in his very informative bulletin, *Global Minds for an Air World:*

"We are going to have to get used to neighbors not only with different colored skins and with different religions, but neighbors speaking different languages.

We are a one-language country. American travelers are embarrassed on finding that so many other peoples speak several languages. We are probably the only major country in the world whose educated class speaks only one language–their mother tongue. This is a real problem for airlines and other business firms who are trying to staff their offices in several countries. Where are they going to find American employees who can speak several languages? A business representative can't say to a prospective customer, 'If you only knew English, I have something good I could sell you.' We must learn other languages if we are going to have a place of leadership in the world, either commercial or political."

The same thought was expressed by Alex J. Wertis, Personnel Director of the United States Steel Export Company:

"The ability to speak or to learn a foreign language is a tremendous asset. The greatest criticism of Americans in foreign lands in the past has been their reluctance to meet other peoples half-way about language. Other peoples take as much pride in their language and culture as we do in ours. To address them in their own speech is a compliment to their language and culture. It gives you a headstart in personal relations. I do not have to tell you about the success that the Army and Navy have had in teaching languages, even English."

H. W. Burch of the United Press Association, New York, summarizing the need of a foreign language equipment for world journalism, writes:

"There are, in fact, so many visible opportunities for the bilingual or trilingual person that no persuasion should be needed for the aspiring student or adult to perfect himself in a foreign language."

L. B. Morgan, Manager Export Sales, Colorado Fuel & Iron Corporation, New York, stresses the importance of Spanish:

> "There is indeed a vital need in export organizations for young people with a knowledge of a foreign language. Because of the preponderance of trade with Latin America in our export department, a thorough knowledge of Spanish in all its phases is absolutely *de rigueur*. Apart from the practical consideration of this question affecting individual organizations in the conduct of their business, there is the cultural factor which, in the mounting interest in international affairs, should receive greater emphasis. It is obvious that a knowledge of languages fosters good will and understanding which in the long run will redound to our national interest."

It must be stressed, however, that, with the exception of interpreting and translating, the majority of business positions require a technical knowledge within a given field. The manager of the Industrial Relations Department of the International Harvester Co. says:

> ". . . the knowledge of a foreign language is an asset, but of minor consideration as it must be used in conjunction with a specialized trade or profession, such as documentation clerk, bilingual stenographer, diplomatic clerk, etc. These latter functions set the salary more so than the knowledge of a foreign language. When we at Harvest are considering a person for foreign service, the fact that he can speak a foreign language is considered only when all other requirements have been met. This means a clear understanding of Harvester management and sales policies, and expertness in a particular line, such as manufacturing, engineering, and knowledge of the functions of our products."

Esther Newman of the Pan American Broadcasting Company writes:

> "From time to time, we do require the services of individuals with reading and writing capabilities in French, Spanish, and German in both our secretarial and bookkeeping departments. I would recommend, based on our experience, that business usage should be included in the foreign language curriculum in the schools. We have found that, given the best training in the world and with the utmost competence on the part of the student, without a grounding in the business usage of the language involved—particularly financial—students are inadequately prepared to use their foreign language knowledge in the business world."

Charles C. Mentzer, Manager of Personnel, International General Electric Company, writes:

> "The International General Electric Company has representation in practically every country of the free world . . . With this wide range of contact, we have certain positions where competence in a foreign language by employees is absolutely essential in order to perform the work required. . . .
>
> "Probably the most prevalent language for our purposes is Spanish. Portuguese, French, and German are being required more often . . . employees must first have technical competence to perform the work, thus the knowledge of a language is placed second or third in importance in our selection process. . . . In a number of positions, our secretaries are required to take dictation in a foreign language. . . . In field positions, such as sales, product service, engineering, application engineering, and manufacturing, the ability for a person to converse in the required language is most important. . . ."

Stephen A. Schoff, Vice President, Personnel, Pepsi-Cola International, writes:

> "Insofar as our overseas operations are concerned, bilingual ability is almost a prerequisite other than in areas where English is the predominant language, i.e., Australia or parts of Africa. Anyone assigned abroad to any other area definitely would need Spanish, French, German, or Urdu, as the case might be. We generally look for a prospective employee who has a college education, marketing background, and some previous industry experience, in addition to a language ability."

Robert L. Michelson, Assistant to the Vice President of Honeywell, Inc., expresses similar thoughts. This company has plants in Canada, Scotland, and Holland, and subsidiaries in Sweden, Belgium, Switzerland, France, Mexico, and Puerto Rico.

> "The ability to speak and write a foreign language is indeed an asset but is not a necessity for someone who works in international operations in the United States. However, if that person is transferred to a foreign country to head up one of our subsidiaries, for example, then it becomes important that he learn to communicate fluently in the language of that country."

The last statement is, of course, very encouraging to those with linguistic training.

THE USEFULNESS OF LANGUAGES IN BUSINESS

During 1975 the State of Wyoming and the U.S. Office of Education sponsored a study of the language requirements of the current business and industrial labor market in the U.S. The following tables show the numbers of foreign-language speaking individuals employed by the companies surveyed, and the significance of the types of proficiency required.

Table I

Companies surveyed		5,640
No. of responses		1,261
Total employees reported		7,084,383

Employees required use of		Percent
foreign language as:		
a) primary tool	1,000	14
b) secondary tool	11,751	17
c) Not required, but useful	34,651	49
d) Other	4,267	6

Table II

Methods used for meeting language needs by business and industrial firms		Percent
Hire native speakers	393	64.1
Hire college trained or formally trained	308	50.2
Used in-house training	105	17.1
Commercial language schools	287	46.8
Other	33	5.4
Total response	613	

Table III

Hiring practices of business and industry by

proficiency level	No. of employees
Native fluency	74,726
Limited conversation	61,187
Write	65,571
Read and understand	63,046
Translate	5,734
Other	5,446

The businesses and industries reported the need of users of nine languages, with needs for Spanish ranking highest, in the following order: Spanish, French, German, Portuguese, Italian, Japanese, Arabic, Russian, Chinese.

RETURNS TO BE EXPECTED

The salaries paid to persons who use a foreign language vocationally depends, of course, on the degree of skill and the technical knowledge involved. Competence in a language may range all the way from that of a librarian who can identify titles of books in three or four languages, to that of an editor who writes technical articles in French or Spanish; from that of the interpreter who is required to ask only a set of simple, standardized questions, to that of the U.N. expert who has to turn outbursts of emotionally high-strung foreign delegates into correct, idiomatic English. For the ordinary business job it may be said that the average office worker earns from $25 to $50 more per week because of a knowledge of a foreign language. The top salary of a Foreign Service officer, with competency in two foreign languages, is $36,000.

Emilio Mayer, a leading official of the Banca Commerciale Italiana, says:

> "Personnel with a thorough knowledge of foreign languages are generally much better paid. They occupy key positions and, inasmuch as they are hard to replace, they are usually the last ones to be dismissed in the event of a reduction in personnel."

In short, then, it may be said that, since knowledge of a foreign language is an added asset, it will be reflected in additional compensation, comparatively modest in the case of the office workers, and considerable in the case of the highly responsible executive.

The wide range in salaries is immediately apparent when one scans the want-ads. In one column, one reads:

> SPANISH/ENG SECRETARY $215
> No Fee. Top oil importer seeks
> bilingual secretary w/good skills.
> Very diverse.
>
> BANKING, INTERNATIONAL
> Major West Coast Bank seeks int'l
> deputy manager. Candidate must
> have experience in Latin America.
> Fluent Spanish Title AVP or
> VP Salary $25-$30,000.

It all depends on the training and experience of the applicant.

ATTRIBUTES NECESSARY FOR SUCCESS

In every line of endeavor there are certain types of native equipment which qualify a person to succeed. This is primarily true of the arts, where a natural gift or talent is essential. One who has no ear for tone can learn to play the piano but he will never become a successful creative musician. One who has no dramatic ability will fail on the stage; without a voice you cannot sing.

In certain respects the same holds true for language. Every normal human being can learn a foreign tongue, but only those who possess particular mental traits will do so with ease and will use the language with skill. Such traits constitute what we may term "linguistic ability."

One of the primary phases of language learning is the acquisition and retention of a large stock of words and idioms; hence, the importance of memory. But even the possession of an extensive vocabulary does not make one a speaker or writer in the foreign tongue. The words must be combined correctly in sentences and thought groups for specific situations; hence, the importance of imagination.

Since oral expression is necessarily rapid, the mental processes must be almost instantaneous; the quick thinker is also the more effective speaker and writer. Learning the printed language is helped by a sense of logical sequence and analogy. Learning the spoken tongue is greatly facilitated by imitativeness. Children learn to speak almost exclusively by means of this ability. Persons who possess this gift can repeat correctly entire sentences even in a difficult foreign tongue, despite the fact that they do not know their meaning. Finally, there must be built up, through constant practice, a sense of what is correct and incorrect. It becomes almost instinctive; it is known scientifically as *Sprachgefühl*, or a "feeling for language."

In addition to the mental functions mentioned above, there are also several physical ones. For speaking, the most important one is flexibility and adaptiveness of the vocal organs. Children learn to speak a language with ease because their teeth, tongue, and vocal cords are not yet fixed. Adults experience greater difficulty in speaking a new tongue for this reason and also because for years they have employed only certain mouth formations. In this connection, phonetics, which aims to describe sounds and their correct production, is helpful. However, the younger person still has a considerable advantage in learning to speak a foreign language.

Different people possess linguistic faculties in varying degrees. Bernard Shaw knew several European languages but he did not speak them well, although he was a genius in English. On the other hand, many waiters can converse glibly in five or six languages.

A native-born American, even with a very limited knowledge of the foreign language, is offered many opportunities in the business world. Of course, any ambitious and conscientious person, once he has a job, will make every effort to improve his command of the foreign language and thus prepare himself for a higher position.

Overleaf: Training in a foreign language may begin in elementary, secondary, college, or adult education classes. The earlier the training begins, the easier it is to become proficient. (Photo: University of Illinois at Chicago Circle, Chicago, Illinois.)

CHAPTER 2

EDUCATIONAL PREPARATION

Since in many cases the vocational use of a foreign language is combined with some other technical activity—stenography, international trade, engineering, etc.—it is wise to adjust one's educational preparation accordingly. Beginning with secondary education, students should make provision for training in a foreign language. If one plans a career which requires a high degree of technical ability, he will continue his training at a college and possibly at a professional institute. As in all fields, the principle will hold true that the longer the training, the greater the skill; the greater the skill, the higher the salary.

HIGH SCHOOL

In most metropolitan areas throughout the United States, high schools offer the standard languages—French, German, Latin, and Spanish. In addition, because of local conditions and the presence of various nationalities, other languages may also appear in the high school curriculum. Among these are Italian, Portuguese, Hebrew, Norwegian, Hungarian, Polish, and Russian.

High schools usually do not offer more than three years of a foreign language; in rare cases a fourth year is provided. However, there are some larger school systems, like that of New York, where language instruction begins in the eighth year. Also, there are now throughout the country many cities in which a foreign language, generally Spanish or French, is taught in the elementary grades.

It is important for the future linguist to begin his language studies as early as possible. There is nothing more valuable than

American students may study one or more foreign languages in college as a major subject concentration or in combination with another major field such as education, business, social work, or economics.

Photo: University of Illinois at Chicago Circle.

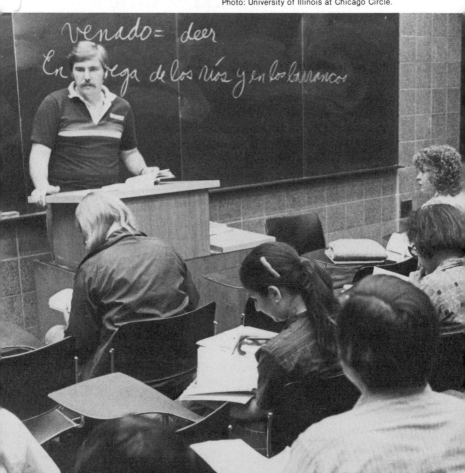

a firm grounding in the language at an early age. There may be some difficulty, especially in smaller communities, in pursuing certain languages. Fortunately, however, the language most in demand in business is also the most widely taught throughout the country—namely, Spanish.

If at all feasible, the young linguist should begin a second language after a year or two of a first one. In order to make good progress, the student should not only do the regular school assignments, but also should take advantage of every opportunity to extend his knowledge of and to get practice in the foreign language, especially in speaking. Some suggestions for additional practice are discussed later on.

COLLEGE

Because of organizational difficulties, it is frequently impossible to continue a language throughout the entire four years of high school. This is most unfortunate, for nothing declines so rapidly without practice as mastery of a language, except perhaps musical skill. Speaking facility in a foreign language deteriorates quickly; reading ability lasts a little longer.

It is important, therefore, to maintain one's language throughout high school—possibly by attending meetings of a language club or sitting as an "auditor" in a language class.

The languages begun in high school should, of course, be continued in college. It is advisable to take as many courses as possible, especially those of a practical nature—scientific German, commercial Spanish, and so on.

THE CHOICE OF A FOREIGN LANGUAGE

What language to pursue in high school depends largely, of course, on the field of work one is planning to enter. For export trade with Latin America it would undoubtedly be Spanish. Frequently, a young person does not know precisely what profession he will enter. In such a case, it is justifiable to follow personal preference or to go according to college requirements. In addition, educational and vocational guidance can be most helpful to students in making wise career choices.

The Massachusetts Institute of Technology, one of the leading institutions in its field, publishes a six-page pamphlet entitled *What Foreign Languages Shall I Study During Secondary School?* Roland B. Greeley, Director of Admissions, makes the following interesting and useful recommendations:

> "The knowledge of foreign languages is always desirable and frequently essential for the future scientist and engineer. Study should begin as early as possible, with the choice of languages dependent on factors which vary according to the individual. . . .
>
> "The study of a foreign language, ancient or modern, broadens the student's cultural and intellectual horizon. In addition to its value in the enrichment of mind and culture, the study of language has practical uses. It furthers commercial, scientific, and social intercourse with foreign countries. Facility in colloquial speech is likely to be of particular value in this kind of work. The United States is developing closer contacts with the rest of the world than ever before. It follows that leaders in every field will increasingly need to be conversant with foreign conditions and foreign tongues. Foreign languages are a necessary part of the training of those who aspire to responsible leadership. American engineers, scientists, architects, and executives are likely to have increasing need for oral language proficiency in order to compete with professionals of other countries, who have a long tradition of language facility.

"Another practical reason for language study concerns the specialized purposes of research. It is true that many practicing engineers in this country— for example, those concerned with construction, industrial production, management, accounting or domestic marketing as these activities relate to technology—have little or no professional need for a foreign language. On the other hand, those whose work involves research or design problems of a fundamental nature need to be in constant touch with developments in other countries. Most scientific and technical reports, periodicals, and other documents, including patents, are not available in translation. It follows that at least a reading knowledge of several foreign languages is important for the research scientist or engineer."

The study of foreign languages should, in general, commence as early in life as possible.

What Language to Study. There is no quick and easy answer to the question: "What language shall I study?" The answer must take into account the individual student's tastes and interests, the educational opportunites available to him, and his probable future field of work. Perhaps the most helpful approach to the question will be a brief discussion of the languages which are likely to be important to a future scientist or engineer.

German. There is in German a considerable backlog of scientific literature to which access is important for the research worker. Many scientific reports from the countries of Central Europe and Scandinavia have been published in German. The language therefore has a scientific significance which goes beyond the cultural contributions of Germany itself.

French. In general, the French are at their best in treating the sciences in their pure or theoretical aspects. In many of these areas, French thought is preeminent. There exists in French an important scientific literature, particularly in biology, mathematics, physics, and chemistry.

Russian. The new position of Russia as the second great scientific nation of the world after the U.S. indicates that its language will continue to increase in general currency as well as in scientific use.

In such fields as aerodynamics, electronics, mathematics, metallurgy, nuclear science and engineering, and theoretical physics, Russian publications are second in importance only to those in English. Inability to keep abreast of Russian development is a severe handicap. America needs many more people trained in reading technical Russian, not to mention the equally great need for competent speakers of that language.

Other languages. Looking ahead to the probable future complexion of the world, it appears that Chinese and Arabic will assume much greater importance for Americans. Other languages, such as Italian, Spanish, and Japanese, may be of interest to scientists in certain special fields.

THE DECISION IS YOURS

The future engineer or scientist, planning his high school course, may well proceed as follows: if he has ties with or interest in a particular foreign country, or if he plans to take up work leading to such an interest, then he should try to make an early start on the appropriate language. In the absence of any such specific interest, he should consider whether his inclinations will lead him into research or fundamental work. He should make a choice of a particular language for study depending on the type of work he intends to pursue and, of course on the availability of instruction.

On the average, three years of study of a language in secondary school is the minimum required to assure knowledge which will persist over the following few years. Four years is better—a thorough knowledge of one foreign language will be more valuable than a smattering of two different languages.

GETTING PRACTICE

Learning a language thoroughly requires time, patience, and practice. It cannot be done solely in school; with the large classes the opportunity for practice consists of but a few minutes daily for the individual student. It is as with the learning of the violin; it is not the one lesson a week that counts in the acquisition of dexterity, but the hours of practice before and after the lesson. In the case of language learning, particularly, there must be what the psychologists call "over-learning" so that responses become practically automatic.

The earnest language student will try to do additional reading. Annotated editions of the classics are very helpful, that is, school editions provided with notes and vocabularies. These can be bought secondhand; progressive schools and language departments will have some in their libraries.

A fruitful source of up-to-date vocabulary for the more advanced student is the foreign magazine and the foreign language newspaper. Newspapers from abroad can be subscribed to or obtained from certain newsdealers. In most metropolitan areas, dailies and weeklies are published in foreign languages. In New York, for instance, there are such in French, German, Italian, Spanish, Portuguese, Russian, Polish, Norwegian, Arabic, Yiddish, Greek, and Czech.

There are a number of excellent magazines published in foreign languages. The Pan American Union in Washington issues its bulletin in French, Spanish, and Portuguese. There is the universally known *Reader's Digest,* which comes in 26 editions in 12 different languages. Since it contains articles on every conceivable subject, it is a gold mine for technical expressions, idioms, and new colloquialisms. The student should record these in a notebook and try to use them.

Listening to the spoken language is excellent practice. This can be done conveniently with the radio and with the phonograph. In many metropolitan areas, there are usually a number of stations which broadcast programs in foreign languages. In New York, for example, Italian, Yiddish, German, Polish, and Spanish may be heard daily.

The phonograph record is also helpful and there are several companies which specialize in foreign language records. Of course, most of the records are for beginning students, but there are also some with dramatic and literary selections spoken by experts. Long-playing records may be obtained which contain entire plays by Racine, Corneille, and Moliere. These provide excellent models for correct pronunciation and intonation. In addition to records, discs, and tapes, and inexpensive cassettes also are available.

SPECIAL TRAINING

A high school course of three or four years in a language, together with the business training given in the commercial department, will suffice for an office job. However, college training is advisable for higher positions in business and civil service and is indispensable for teaching and scholarly research. In addition, for the person hoping to become a highly paid executive with a near-native command of a language, there are the Berlitz Schools. They are known all over the world and teach 45 languages. There are 62 schools in the United States and more than 200 in 23 countries on five continents.

Another special school is the Latin American Institute which prepares students primarily for positions requiring Spanish,

Portuguese or French. The Institute will, however, offer German or Russian if there is a sufficient demand. Excellent courses are provided in secretarial work, diplomatic and foreign service, and foreign trade. These courses usually require two years to complete.

One of the best language schools is the Institute of Languages and Linguistics in Washington, D.C., which is part of the School of Foreign Service of Georgetown University. The School is "dedicated to the preparation of men and women for diplomatic and consular service, foreign trade, international shipping, business careers, overseas activities, and public administration." The Institute is "designed to offer specialized instruction to selected candidates whose actual or contemplated professional activities require an effective knowledge of languages." The Institute also does research in applied linguistics and in the field of language methodology. Correlated courses in geography, history, civilization, and contemporary problems are conducted in several major languages, as well as courses in foreign relations, international law, and world economics.

With its elaborate electronic equipment, the Institute provides opportunity for training in simultaneous multilingual translation. The languages used in this system are French, German, English, Spanish, Russian, and Chinese. The school is continually expanding its facilities and now provides instruction in more than 30 languages.

There are numerous summer language schools for teachers. Those maintained abroad by some of the universities and colleges are highly recommended; for example, New York University has summer institutes in six European countries. The tuition is only two-thirds that of the regular rate, and board and lodging are obtainable for less than $5 a day. In three summer sessions a student can acquire enough credits for the master's degree.

In every large city there are language schools, like those of Berlitz, where instruction is given by natives. Of course, the finishing touch of the language student's training is a trip abroad with an extended stay in the country whose language is his specialty.

PREPARATION FOR A BILINGUAL OFFICE JOB

As was stated above, a good high school course in a foreign language and commercial subjects will prepare a young person for an office job. If, however, he is ambitious and wants a more attractive position with a better paying salary, it is advisable for him to take some courses at a recognized business school. In fact, the average businessman much prefers the graduate of a private commercial college to the product of the public high school.

There are, of course, different kinds of positions on various levels. The Latin American Institute trains high school graduates for business, offering the following programs:

> Private Secretary
> Bilingual Secretary
> Diplomatic and Executive Secretary
> Foreign Trade Secretary
> Translator and Interpreter
> Export-Import Traffic Manager
> Intensive Courses for College Graduates

PLANNING YOUR COURSES

Since in most cases the vocational use of a foreign language is combined with some other technical skill—stenography, international trade, engineering, marketing, etc.—it is wise to plan one's educational preparation accordingly. Beginning with secondary education, provision should be made for training in a foreign language and in other major academic subjects. In preparation for a career that requires a high degree of technical skill, advanced courses at a university or professional institute are highly recommended. As in all fields, the principle will hold true that the longer the training, the greater the skill; the greater the skill, the higher the salary.

Studies have been made of the incidence of various college majors in combination with foreign language skill. Ranked in order of frequency, in a recent study, they included: business adm./mgt., marketing/sales, engineering, secretarial skills, finance, international relations, accounting, economics, clerical skills, communications, law, public relations, advertising, data processing, English language skills, civil engineering, journalism, area studies, statistics, psychology, library skills, cultural studies, public administration, sociology, political science, and fine arts.

Many major corporations also incorporate foreign language in their training programs and/or hire individuals who have combinations of skills like those listed above. Some of the largest of these corporations are: Exxon, General Motors, Ford Motor Co., Texaco, Mobil, Standard Oil, Gulf Oil, IBM, General Electric, Chrysler, IT&T, Shell Oil, U.S. Steel, Atlantic Richfield, Du Pont (I.E.) de Nemours, Continental Oil, Western Electric, Proctor & Gamble, Tenneco, Union Carbide, Westinghouse Electric, Goodyear Tire & Rubber, and Phillips Petroleum.

PREPARATION FOR GOVERNMENT SERVICE

In preparing for foreign government service, you should broaden your courses to include geography, economics, money and banking, diplomatic correspondence, and international law.

Preparation for the position of foreign service officer should include, in addition to foreign languages, American history and government, international diplomatic protocol, economic and political geography, and consular documents.

Special secretarial training will qualify you for the following jobs: diplomatic secretary, consular assistant, executive secretary, translator, interpreter or bilingual secretary.

The following courses are recommended for the future Foreign Service Officer:

American History	International Law
American Government	Economic and
Diplomatic History	Political Geography
Latin American History	Business English
European History	Diplomatic Correspondence
International Relations	Economics
Money and Banking	Grammar
Remedial Writing	Conversation
English Stenography	Composition
Typewriting	Commercial Correspondence
Foreign Language	Translation Technique

PREPARATION FOR INTERNATIONAL CAREERS

An outstanding institution, specializing in the training of men and women for overseas careers in international commerce or the U.S. Foreign Service, is the American Graduate School of International Management in Glendale, Arizona. College students holding a bachelor's degree are accepted for intensive training in the practical techniques of international commerce; in acquiring an active speaking command of at least one of the major foreign languages; and in general knowledge of selected world areas and ethnic groups.

The degree of Master of International Management (M.I.M.) is awarded upon successful completion of 48 semester hours of work. Special students, or those who do not complete the full requirements for the M.I.M. degree, are given the Certificate of Advanced Study.

Tuition is $1,200 per semester. Spouses of full-time students may take up to nine hours of study per semester at $300 per term. Board at the school is at the rate of $425 per person per semester. Lodging costs $215 or $175 for single students. Suites for married students are available at a rental of $400-$450 per semester. Including all extras, the minimum cost of a regular academic semester for a single student is $1,967 and for married students, $2,627.

There is a generous aid program to help deserving students who need financial assistance. Scholarships are provided by sixteen different organizations, and ten loan funds are available to the students. Help also is given in securing on-campus or off-campus employment.

The curriculum includes every aspect of international trade. The world business courses consist of accounting, managerial economics, operations analysis, management, and marketing. The total 48 hours required include mandatory courses in international studies, world business, and modern languages. In the latter, the requirement is generally 15 hours or 16 for Japanese. Introductory, intermediate, and advanced courses are offered in Chinese, French, German, Japanese, Portuguese, and Spanish.

Graduates of the school have been hired by over 2,600 organizations in both the public and private sector since the founding of the school in 1946. Its directors envision very attractive future careers in the field of international operations, as indicated in the school's bulletin:

> "Total U.S. long-term private investments overseas rose from $49 billion to around $120 billion over the past decade. Foreign direct investments in the U.S. have passed the $14 billion mark; and in addition, corporate portfolio investments on the part of foreigners, in the form of stocks and bonds, amount to approximately $39 billion. Governmental agencies of all nations, as well as a wide range of non-governmental, social, religious, and educational organizations, are assuming greater and more complex international obligations.

"This rapidly expanding involvement of Americans overseas has created a critical need for executive managerial talent in the fields of marketing, finance, business management, advertising, governmental operations, welfare services, and technical assistance to developing areas. It also has created an urgent need for the training of foreign nationals in American managerial practices and technical skills for application and adaptation to local environments in both home industries and multinational corporations.

"An international career, however, imposes special obligations and requires unusual talents on the part of an individual. Young executives are expected to assume broader and more responsible positions earlier in their careers. . . .

"To meet these special demands imposed on the international manager, a distinctive education is required beyond that offered by the traditional graduate schools of business administration. Such an education places a premium on conversational proficiency in a foreign language in order to enable the executive to communicate directly with his counterparts and subordinates in his work and social relations overseas."

Those preparing for jobs in Asia will, of course, take the Far East Area Studies course, the usual business subjects, and should consider taking French . . . the most likely second language they can expect to encounter over most of that widely-varying territory, especially in Southeast Asia.

Government Service Abroad. This field of specialization includes employment by those civilian agencies of the federal government which are concerned with foreign problems, or employment by international organizations of an official or semipublic nature. The former category includes the Department of State, the U.S. Information Agency, the International Cooperation Administration, the Bureau of Foreign Commerce, and other government agencies.

The course of studies should emphasize area and language studies as well as international relations and presupposes some previous acquaintance with those disciplines.

International Commerce in the United States. This specialization is designed for those who plan a career in foreign trade which will not involve assignment to a foreign country. The excellent opportunities in this field include employment in international divisions, export departments, and foreign departments of financial houses and chambers of commerce . . . in all of these, familiarity with a foreign language is desirable. This specialization includes the following courses:

> Introduction to World Trade
> Financial Operations and Documentation of
>   International Commerce
> Problems of Foreign Trade Procedure
> Research in Foreign Marketing
> Accounting for Management
> Analysis of Financial Statements
> Comparative Accounting Practices
> Advertising Theory and Practice
> Basic Principles of Salesmanship
> International Law of Commerce
> Management; Organizational Structure

The Latin American Institute offers a course in International Trade and one in Foreign Trade Secretary.

Overleaf: Job opportunities for speakers and writers of Arabic have increased rapidly since the early 1970s. (Photo: American Graduate School of International Management.)

CHAPTER 3

FINDING YOUR JOB

As you near completion of your high school or college training, you will be thinking about the possibilities of securing employment. There are, of course, a number of ways to get a job. If you have a relative or a friend who is established in a specific field and who is eager to hire you, that, naturally, is a very happy solution. However, most young people do not have connections and must apply for a position.

Today, the larger high schools and practically all colleges maintain employment bureaus and endeavor to supply their students with vocational guidance. You may be able to secure a position through such an office or, if not a job, at least some helpful suggestions as to how to look for one.

In the case of private secretarial and other specialized schools, there is practically a guarantee that the institution will place you if you have successfully completed the required courses. For example, the Latin American Institute maintains an active placement bureau which makes no charge to student, alumnus or employer. Through this bureau, the Institute secures positions for graduating students and alumni who want to change or better their positions. Contact is made for the student toward the end of his course with organizations or government departments in the chosen field. The student is given instruction in the technique of applying for such positions, and each student is assisted in preparing a mimeographed personal data sheet, giving a detailed record of all past history, personal factors, courses taken, and so on, for submission to potential employers. The placement bureau of the Institute maintains close and personal contact with the personnel divisions of all important business concerns and government offices, who constantly refer to the Institute whenever they need the specialized personnel which frequently only the Latin American Institute trains. The placement bureau of the school thus offers a lifetime service, and any former student of the Institute may depend upon the full cooperation of the bureau at any time.

HELP WANTED

To an ordinary person seeking a job, his first thought is to look at the want ads in the daily paper. There is, of course, no more fruitful general source of employment opportunities. As shown in a previous chapter, the Sunday edition of *The New York Times* publishes about ninety advertisements of positions for which some knowledge of a foreign language is required.

WRITING THE LETTER OF APPLICATION

The letter applying for a position should be composed and written with great care, for your application may compete with hundreds of others. Each applicant will be judged by his handwriting, the correctness of his English, the ease of his style, and the contents of his letter. The following are a few helpful suggestions:

● If possible, address an individual in the firm, using his full name and correct title.

● Instead of implying that you are looking for a job, offer your services.

- Indicate that you know what the job is about and that you are genuinely interested.

- Show that your previous experience has prepared you for the job.

- Be specific about your qualifications and the results you have obtained in the past.

- Make your letter stand out by personal description; avoid anything stereotyped.

- Try to have an effective opening sentence and a strong closing sentence.

- Avoid hackneyed and stereotyped phrases; write naturally and sincerely, but be modest in expressing opinions.

- Check your letter for errors in grammar, spelling and punctuation.

- Remember, "Brevity is the soul of wit." Strike out unecessary words and phrases; do not repeat yourself.

- Mention two or three references. In addition to their addresses, give their telephone numbers, if possible.

- If you have a good letter of reference, you might type it or mimeograph it and enclose a copy in your letter of application.

PERSONAL INTERVIEW

If you are called for a personal interview, your aim, of course, will be to make as good an impression as possible. The two major factors in any application for a job are competency and personality. The former is largely a matter of training and intelligence and reveals itself best on the job. Even if the personnel manager should go to the trouble of giving you a test, he will not discover all your potentialities.

Actually, in applying for a position you are judged primarily on the basis of personality. This consists of a combination of such factors as appearance, health, poise, manners, and speech. Although the attire of many people, including that of executives and public figures, has taken on an air of casualness, when applying for a job, it is still prudent to be neat and well-groomed.

The personal traits generally rated highest in a candidate are intelligence, accuracy, good judgment, efficiency, loyalty, adaptiveness, and executive ability. The employer may ask questions in an endeavor to determine whether or not you possess some of the above qualities.

EMPLOYMENT AGENCIES

There are a great number of employment agencies, especially in large cities, but only a few of them specialize in jobs with foreign language requirements. The agency, of course, charges a fee for securing the job for the applicant. In many cases, however, the employer will take care of this expense, and often, this fact is stated in the want ad.

In addition to the commercial agencies, there are various government offices through which employment may be obtained, including the state employment services. Federal employment is taken care of by the Civil Service Commission which maintains offices in principal cities.

EMPLOYMENT ABROAD

When you seek a position in the export field, the question frequently arises: will you work in the home office or in foreign countries? Some firms, like W.R. Grace & Co., prepare their young employees or, at least, a limited number of them, for service in Latin America. A knowledge of Spanish is, of course, of great importance. We must not, however, forget Brazil, one of the largest buyers in South America of American goods, whose language is Portuguese. Some of the large U.S. business houses doing business in that country are: Standard Oil, U.S. Steel, General Electric, General Motors, Ford Motor Co., Lilly Pharmaceutical Co., Coca Cola, and National City Bank. A major portion of the executives and technical experts of these companies are Americans.

It is of interest, too, to note what qualifications are required in connection with higher positions in the export field and what jobs are available. The advertisements given below are taken from *The Exporter,* a trade journal:

Far Eastern Representative

"Leading manufacturer of well-known industrial products seeks sales representative for Far East. Substantial opportunity exists for person with capabilities to eventually assume complete responsibility for sales, licensing, and investment program now under way in the area. This is a career position involving indefinite foreign residence and considerable travel. Applicants must have work experience in foreign trade, mature judgment, and ability to plan own work program and carry it out effectively without constant direction from headquarters. Submit complete resume, photograph, salary requirements, and letter stating why you qualify for this position."

POSITIONS WANTED

Export Sales Manager

"Will help to establish or increase your export sales. Top experience export marketing and manufacturing. Intimate knowledge Latin American (18 years' residence) and European markets.

Fluent Spanish, German, French, and others. Willing part-time travel from New York City base. European college degree. Seeks challenging export sales position."

Foreign Consultant, Associate

"Aggressive American executive with Swiss background and training, 30 years' experience in foreign business, international trade, and establishing organizations overseas, available as consultant or full-time associate. Speaks several languages fluently. Wide administrative and sales experience in Far East, Europe, Canada, Africa, and U.S.A."

SECURING A JOB IN SOUTH AMERICA

For those interested in obtaining a position in a South American country, the following information will be valuable. It is taken from a report prepared several years ago by J. Silvado Bueno of the Foreign Trade Office, Pan American Union, Washington, D.C.:

"United States citizens who wish to work in Latin America are advised to seek employment with North American firms. Some outstanding reasons for this follow:

(a) the guarantee of work, before departing from the United States, provided by a contract with such a firm.

(b) the advantage of salary payment, usually in dollars, or half in dollars and half in the currency of the country in which one is to work.

(c) the 'cost of living allowance' where living costs are highly inflated. (This seems to be a general policy among United States companies.)

(d) the possibility that the candidate for work

has not had an opportunity to become proficient in Spanish, Portuguese or French, and this deficiency may not constitute an insurmountable barrier when he is employed by a North American concern.

"Attention is called to the fact that openings in Latin America are generally limited in scope and number. While there are some opportunities for those trained in bilingual or trilingual stenography and typing, the greatest need is for specialists in administration, management, engineering, sanitation, and transportation. There is a demand for experts in agricultural methods, industry, and aviation. North Americans may obtain jobs in these fields, for which there are few qualified natives. Candidates for these jobs must be highly trained and supported by adequate documentation; they must offer acceptable recommendations. Professional degrees and some years of practical experience are usually indispensable for successful consideration.

"On the other hand, United States firms have often adopted the policy of training nationals for technical and management positions . . . because of the need to conform to labor laws in these countries which stipulate that most of the employees in designated industries be native-born or naturalized citizens.

"Our suggestions include the absolute need of a solid knowledge of Spanish and/or Portuguese. The importance of this requirement should not be minimized. Candidates, however, are warned against assuming that knowledge of languages alone will guarantee success in Latin America.

"College graduates, particularly those with professional training or experience, have found employment in Latin America through the following agencies, depending on major interest:

● Division of Overseas Information Centers, Department of State, Washington, D.C. Positions may be obtained for the teaching of English, library, supervisory, and administrative work abroad.

● United States citizens may work abroad as members of the Foreign Service (Department of State). The officers in this service are required to be familiar with the civilization and language of the country to which they are sent.

● Specialists may obtain foreign assignments when employed by the United States Department of Agriculture, U.S. Department of Commerce, and the U.S. Justice Department.

● Hundreds of United States firms maintain branches in most Latin American countries. This office (Pan American Union) supplies partial lists of these for many countries. Candidates are urged to write directly to these firms."

BUSINESS OPENINGS

One of the best portals of entry to an attractive business career is by way of a secretaryship. Bilingual secretaries are in wide demand in various branches of commerce and of international relations. Large business concerns, airlines, banks, and international organizations maintain foreign departments in which personnel trained in one or a number of foreign languages are needed. The work is interesting and the remuneration is always higher than that paid to the ordinary secretary. Furthermore, advancement from a secretaryship to higher positions is rapid.

Closely related to this field are the following types of positions, which are also open to those with a bilingual secretarial training: export assistant, assistant foreign credit manager, trade analyst, correspondent, consular invoice clerk, assistant traffic manager, and executive assistant. In recent years, the languages most in demand in connection with these positions have been Spanish, French, and Portuguese.

With the rapidly increasing commercial relations of the United States, there is probably no field today which offers greater opportunity to those who have the training than the import-export field. The pay is good, the work is interesting, and there are often opportunities for travel.

GOVERNMENT POSITIONS

Aside from positions with commercial concerns, there is a wide variety of interesting activities in the fields of diplomacy and foreign service. The remuneration is good and there are many possibilities for rapid advancement.

The United States government regularly schedules examinations to supply personnel for the foreign offices of the Departments of State and of Commerce. There are interesting and remunerative positions as foreign service officers and thousands of jobs as clerks or stenographers in embassies and consulates of the United States for those who know two languages. Generally, a college education is not required for the latter positions, and women are accepted on the same basis as men.

The Bureau of Labor Statistics of the U.S. Department of Labor issues a folder entitled "Foreign Languages and Your Career." Attention is drawn to the following areas in which knowledge of a foreign language is useful—clerical, tourism, marketing, finance, engineering, and government. In answer to the question, "Which Language Should You Study?" the following statement is made: " . . . the most needed languages are Spanish, French, and German, followed by Portuguese, Italian, Japanese and Chinese."

The Bureau also publishes the *Occupational Outlook Handbook* that contains information on occupations in which "command of a foreign language is either necessary or useful." More than thirty occupations are listed. For each one a reprint is available. Some of the more important of these and their numbers of the reprints are:

Bookkeeping Workers	No. 1875-15	Environmental Scientists	No. 1875- 76
Secretaries, Steno-graphers, Typists	No. 1875-22	Biochemists	No. 1875- 77
Banking: Bank Officers, Tellers, Clerks	No. 1875-24	Physical Scien-tists, Chemists, Physicists	No. 1875- 79
Advertising, Marketing Research	No. 1875-27	Physicians	No. 1875-102
Buyers	No. 1875-28	Nurses; Practi-cal	No. 1875-106
Teachers: Elementary, Secondary and College	No. 1875-48	Therapists	No. 1875-107
		Social Scien-tists	No. 1875-113
Librarians, Library Technicians & Assistants	No. 1875-49	Clergy	No. 1875-116
		Social Workers	No. 1875-119
Civil Aviation: Pilots, Passenger Agents	No. 1875-69	Actors, Singers	No. 1875-120
Engineers: Civil, Mining	No. 1875-75	Newspaper Reporters	No. 1875-129
		Interpreters	No. 1875-130

When ordering reprints, the identifying number should be given. The reprints may be obtained for a small fee at any of the regional offices of the Bureau of Labor Statistics, U.S. Department of Labor.

1603 Federal Office Bldg.   230 South Dearborn St.
Boston, Mass. 02203   Chicago, Ill. 60604

1515 Broadway   911 Walnut St.
New York, N.Y. 10036   Kansas City, Mo. 64106

P.O. Box 13309
Philadelphia, Pa. 19101

555 Griffin Sq. Bldg.
Dallas, Tex. 75202

1371 Peachtree St. N.E.
Atlanta, Ga. 30309

450 Golden Gate Ave., Box 36017
San Francisco, Cal. 94102

The *Occupational Outlook Handbook* (BLS Bulletin No. 1875) may also be purchased from the regional offices at approximately $7.00 a copy. Current prices will be quoted on request by any of the offices.

ANALYSIS OF THE JOB

If you have succeeded in getting several job offers, each of which may seem attractive, the difficult question is: which one shall you accept? To make a wise choice, you will have to analyze the demands of the job and to evaluate, objectively, your own fitness and eagerness for it. Temperaments and interests differ and you may be much happier in one position than another.

Of basic importance is knowing exactly what you are expected to do, especially with reference to your linguistic ability. As stated before, competency in a foreign language is on various levels, ranging all the way from a so-called "smattering" (which may be useful on a lower level), to a high degree of technical skill.

In help wanted advertisements the designations most frequently used are "knowledge," "knowledge desirable," "knowledge helpful," "speak," "fluent command," and "can take dictation." As indicated previously, the largest number of office jobs fall under "dictation" and "knowledge."

TYPES OF POSITIONS

Some of the positions for which a young person who has had commercial training and knows a foreign language may qualify are the following:

Bilingual stenographer	Bookkeeper
Consular invoice clerk	Assistant trade analyst
Export assistant	Interpreter

One step higher is that of private secretary. The bilingual stenographer who has taken courses in economics, banking, and law can qualify for:

Office manager	Executive assistant
Traffic assistant	Assistant production manager
Personnel director	Interviewer
Correspondent secretary	Public relations secretary

The last mentioned, that is, public relations, opens up a very broad and attractive field. Related positions are:

International public relations secretary	Educational public relations secretary
Publicity assistant	Industrial relations secretary
Public opinion analyst	Consumer public relations director
Individual campaign public relations secretary	

The most important commercial field for the person with foreign language training is, of course, export-import. Attractive positions are:

Export manager	International traveling agent
Assistant manager of foreign department	Air traffic assistant
	Executive secretary
Supervisor, export department	Trade analyst
	Resident buyer
Foreign purchasing agent	Foreign field researcher
Traffic manager	Foreign raw materials buyer
Foreign credit manager	Translator

Then there are the positions for representatives stationed abroad:

Business manager	Foreign personnel director
Foreign markets analyst	Export purchasing agent
Resident buyer	Foreign credit manager

Finally, there are various government positions, here and abroad, which require a knowledge of foreign languages:

Diplomatic secretary	Foreign service officer
Consular assistant	Interpreter
Foreign markets analyst	Foreign representative
Raw material analyst	

YOUR DUTIES ON THE JOB

The duties required of you in connection with your work in foreign languages will, of course, depend upon the nature of the business or organization of which you are a part and also upon the responsibilities of your immediate superior.

Since most young people enter an organization via an office job, let us consider the duties of the stenographer and secretary. The distinction between the two is not always clearly drawn. Secretary means confidential officer and assumes that the knowledge and skills required are above that of the ordinary clerk.

The most important general duties that are required of the average bilingual secretary are the following:

- The taking of dictation and the transcribing of shorthand notes. In the case of the bilingual secretary, this means, of course, use of the foreign language when required.
- Composing and writing original letters in English and in the foreign language.

- Receiving callers; acting as interpreter.
- Handling incoming mail, answering letters, and noting information in letters.
- Organizing office routine.
- Organizing filing systems.
- Consulting reference works.
- Making appointments.
- Taking care of telephone calls.
- Keeping minutes of staff and executive meetings.
- Dictating letters.
- Preparing reports and translating material.

The activities of a translator are, of course, quite different. Since all his work will be written, the ability to type is definitely an asset. There will hardly be any need for spoken fluency. On the other hand, especially in the more technical fields of advertising, the resourcefulness of the translator is important. He may even have to coin new words and expressions.

Translating falls into various categories. It may consist of reproducing literary material in English. If novels or essays are involved, the translator must possess some literary skill. Or, it may be merely a matter of translating ordinary news dispatches.

Then again, the material may consist of highly technical language, such as legal, medical, pharmaceutical, chemical or engineering articles. The furnishing of abstracts is one of the duties of the average translator. The ordinary commercial translation bureau must be prepared for anything, including poorly written and badly phrased material. The more highly paid translators are those who translate English advertising copy into foreign languages.

The interpreter, too, may work on different levels. At the bottom of the scale is the court interpreter; at the top is the highly gifted U.N. linguist whose ingenuity is constantly being called upon. His effectiveness, of course, depends essentially upon oral fluency.

Oral fluency, too, is involved in all positions requiring personal contacts such as in social work, the hotel and travel business, and nursing.

Overleaf: Foreign trade has stimulated increased need for knowledge of Japanese. (Photo: American Graduate School of International Management.)

しんぶんをかいたいん
ですが、どこにあり
ますか。
えきのまえにあります。

CHAPTER 4

OPPORTUNITIES IN FOREIGN TRADE

In connection with vocational opportunities in languages, one thinks primarily of commercial relations with foreign countries, that is, the import-export field. And it is true that in this area, some of the most interesting and lucrative positions are to be found.

Linguistic training is important not only for correspondence and negotiation, but even more so for sales promotion and publicity. In view of the rapid expansion of radio and television usage for communication, propaganda, and advertising in recent years, a vast territory in which foreign languages play a major role has been opened.

That linguistic training is an undeniable asset in this field is affirmed by Lorimer B. Slocum, Director, International Division, Young & Rubicam, one of the largest advertising firms in the United States:

> "The future looks fairly good. This means that more and more Americans will be needed, both at home and abroad, to serve as salesmen, technicians, teachers, public relations emissaries, trouble shooters, etc. This means that the people of other countries will get to know us better as time goes by, will understand us better, and we hope, like us better.
>
> "Students will ask you, 'Is it necessary to learn foreign languages?' Maybe they don't *have to,* but

they will have a lot more fun if they do, and they will find it easier to achieve their goals. They should remember that the more of a language they know and the more they use it, the friendlier will be their reception . . .

"Yes, there are fine opportunities in the international field for our bright, young, ambitious students and their fresh outlook on life. Their up-to-the-minute information on all branches of business and learning could bring not only a breath of fresh air to near and far places, but also give them a broader outlook on life, while they are doing a good deed for their country."

Words like these, coming from an expert, are extremely encouraging to any young person who plans to enter international trade.

ADVERTISING

With America's international trade approximately $105 billion yearly, the worldwide coverage of the best markets through research and advertising is of the utmost importance. In fact, it is so basic to the success of foreign trade that the field of export advertising has been growing by leaps and bounds.

Export Trade has printed a Directory of Foreign Publications which have representatives in the United States. About 600 foreign newspapers and magazines are listed, representing the following languages: Spanish, Portuguese, Dutch, French, German, Italian, Hebrew, Norwegian, Swedish, Turkish, and Hindi.

The same trade journal also provides a list of 105 *U.S. Publications Whose Principal Circulation is in Foreign Countries.* These include technical magazines on antibiotics, automobiles, beverages, office equipment, motion pictures, farm implements, pharmaceutics, engineering, oil, mechanics, textiles, and 26 international foreign language editions of *Reader's Digest.*

It can readily be seen that the field of export advertising offers great opportunities for those with foreign language training.

EXPORT

The world trade of the United States has been increasing by leaps and bounds. According to figures prepared by the International Economic Analysis Division of the Department of Commerce, merchandising exports and imports have been rising almost steadily for the last twenty-five years.

American commerce and business penetrate even the most distant areas of the globe. The American Graduate School of International Management, which prepares men and women for high-level jobs abroad, published an eight-page folder several years ago listing numerous graduates of the Institute in the following countries:

Afghanistan	Costa Rica
Angola	Denmark
Argentina	Dominican Republic
Australia	Ecuador
Austria	El Salvador
Bahamas	England
Barbados	Formosa
Belgian Congo	France
Belgium	French Equatorial Africa
Bolivia	Germany
Brazil	Ghana
Burma	Greenland
Canada	Guatemala
Canal Zone	Haiti
Chile	Honduras
Colombia	Hong Kong

India
Indonesia
Iran
Iraq
Italy
Jamaica
Japan
Kenya
Korea
Lebanon
Liberia
Madagascar
Malaya
Mariana Islands
Mexico
Morocco
Nepal
Netherlands
Netherlands West Indies
Nicaragua
Nigeria
Norway
Okinawa

Pakistan
Panama
Paraguay
Peru
Philippine Islands
Portugal
Puerto Rico
St. Lucia
Singapore
South Africa
South Rhodesia
South Vietnam
Spain
Sweden
Switzerland
Syria
Thailand
Trinidad
Turkey
Uruguay
Venezuela
Virgin Islands

For Venezuela alone, 48 American firms are listed which employ alumni of the Institute. Among them are such well-known concerns as: Heinz, Chase Manhattan Bank, Continental Emsco, Firestone International, First National Bank, Ford Motor Co., General Tire Co., Goodyear International Corp., International General Electric Co., Minneapolis-Honeywell Regulator Co., Otis Elevator Co., Procter & Gamble, Sears Roebuck, Sinclair Oil.

The following chart published by the U.S. Department of Commerce lists the major foreign powers with which we trade, and value in millions of dollars of the exports and imports. This trade involves millions of workers with foreign language skills.

UNITED STATES Foreign Trade with Leading Countries (1976)
(value in millions of dollars)

	Imports	Exports
Canada	$26,827	$24,109
Denmark	1,131	2,991
France	2,541	3,449
West Germany	5,700	5,730
Ireland	178	280
Italy	2,544	3,068
United Kingdom	3,773	4,799
Greece	146	591
Turkey	223	451
Austria	242	197
Norway	647	500
Portugal	157	400
Sweden	926	1,036
Switzerland	1,041	1,173
Soviet bloc	867	3,502
Asia	39,665	30,257
Japan	15,683	10,144
Africa	12,544	4,396

As can be seen from the above tabulation, our largest foreign trade is with English-speaking countries. Among the others, Japan ranks one of the highest. This would lead to the assumption that Japanese is a very useful language for a business career. The fact is, however, that there are few calls for young Americans who can speak that language, since most professionally active Japanese are well-trained in English.

In Europe, our trade is greatest with Britain, Germany, and France. It would seem then that the most important languages for candidates for European positions in the export and import trade are German and French.

As far as the various continents are concerned, our trade is heaviest with countries in the western hemisphere, with the Latin American countries ranking very high. It is no wonder, then, that there are many calls for young people with competence in Spanish and, to a lesser degree, Portuguese.

The spread of American big business throughout the world is phenomenal. According to *Fortune,* of the world's largest industrial concerns, 24 are based in the United States and ten of the top ones are American. Three of these are automobile manufacturers, including General Motors, Ford, and Chrysler.

The 24 American companies account for 17 percent of the total net income. Besides the U.S., only seven other countries are represented: Germany, Britain, Japan, Italy, France, Switzerland, and Holland. The leading companies are:

	Sales	Net Income
	(in millions)	
General Motors	$35,798	$2,398
Exxon	25,724	2,443
Ford	23,015	907
Royal Dutch-Shell	18,672	1,789
Chrysler	11,774	255
General Electric	11,575	585
Texaco	11,407	1,292
Mobil Oil	11,390	849
Unilever	11,010	423
IBM	10,993	1,575
ITT	10,183	528
Gulf Oil	8,417	800

According to the Statistical Abstract of the United States 1973, issued by the U.S. Department of Commerce, international investments have grown phenomenally.

U.S. Assets Abroad (in billions of dollars)

1950	1955	1960	1965	1970	1971
54.4	65.1	85.6	120.4	166.9	180.6

Our trade with Latin America is constantly growing. In 1976 our exports to 19 American republics amounted to almost $14 billion and our imports to over $11 billion.

Other trade outlets were:

	Exports		Imports	
	1972	1973	1972	1973
19 American Republics	6,467	8,921	5,772	7,790
Central American Common Market	439	621	485	685
Latin Amer. Free Trade Association	5,576	7,708	4,949	6,688
Dominican Republic	183	229	232	307
Panama	216	286	55	67
Bahamas	144	208	247	286
Jamaica	221	268	181	176
Netherlands Antilles	122	159	400	733
Trinidad and Tobago	121	133	251	409

As we have said in the preceding pages, Spanish and Portuguese are extremely important in the field of export trade. H. F. Wiggs, Personnel Director, Ebasco International Corporation, writes:

> "Our major need for young people to go to Latin America to participate in our operations is,

first, for engineers—electrical, mechanical, and civil—
and, second, for accountants."

The "Statistical Abstract of the United States 1973" issued
by the U.S. Department of Commerce gives the following figures
for some of the Latin American countries (in millions of dollars):

	Exports	Imports
Argentina	400	201
Bolivia	45	26
Brazil	1243	942
Chile	187	83
Colombia	317	284
Mexico	1982	1632
Venezuela	924	1298

The steady growth in Latin American trade is reflected in
the following figures, taken from the same report.

Exports (in millions of dollars)

	1960	1972
Central American Common Market	216	439
Latin American Free Trade Association	2978	5580

Imports (in millions of dollars)

	1960	1972
Central American Common Market	180	485
Latin American Free Trade Association	2838	4949

That Spanish is of pre-eminent importance in export is immediately evident upon examination of the commercial literature in
the field. Of the 96 U.S. publications whose principal circulation
is in foreign countries, no fewer than 48—that is, exactly half—are
issued in Spanish.

As has been pointed out, the policy with reference to staffing foreign branches and subsidiaries differs among various firms. Some assume that their representatives will adapt themselves within a short time to conditions in the foreign country, others subject their foreign representatives to preparatory training before sending them abroad. For the rapid acquisition of a foreign language they may be sent to a Berlitz school at the expense of the firm.

This is the practice of large international concerns like International Business Machines (IBM). According to an official of this firm, only nationals, that is, natives, are employed in their foreign subsidiaries. In Mexico and Chile, for example, they maintain only one American as manager. In Paris there is a staff of only four Americans. Since the foreign representatives are highly cultured and speak English fluently, there is also very little need for bilingual secretaries.

One of the largest and oldest American export houses is W. R. Grace & Co. Its founding and rapid growth is a success story typical of nineteenth century America. In 1850, in Ireland, the 18-year-old William Russell Grace, inspired by seafaring talks of South America, decided to seek his fortune in the land of the Incas. With a group of Irish emigrants he sailed for Callao, Peru, in 1851, and embarked on a business career. It was so successful that he founded W. R. Grace & Co. in 1854. Within a short time this firm achieved preeminence in shipping, banking, air transportation, and manufacturing.

For decades W. R. Grace & Co. was the leading American concern dealing with South America. Within recent years this has changed radically, however, since the firm has withdrawn its major operations from that continent. This was necessitated by a number of unfavorable contingencies but chiefly because of the expropriation of American holdings by the radical governments of Peru and Chile.

The company has transferred its major operations to other parts of the world, dealing with practically every country in Europe. It even does business with the Soviet Union and several of the satellite states. A great volume of business also is done with Australia and Japan.

From a shipping and export house, W. R. Grace has expanded into a number of other fields which include chemically based products and services; consumer, agricultural, and medical products; and the development of natural resources. In 1973 the company's total income was $87.5 million.

The corporation has 74,500 employees. The large majority of these are natives of the country in which they work. Relatively few American executives are stationed abroad. There is, however, a continual shuttling back and forth of analysts and specialists from the U.S. For them, the knowledge of a foreign language is a great asset. Since the firm no longer devotes its main efforts to South America, many other languages beside Spanish and Portuguese are important.

Although there are many positions open to those who have had only a high school or business school education, preference is given to the college graduate for all higher positions. This thought is expressed by D. C. Shirey of the Personnel Department of the Firestone Tire & Rubber Co., Akron, Ohio:

> ". . . There is no question that opportunities are great in our company and in many fields of endeavor where a foreign language facility would be of great assistance.
>
> ". . . There are specific jobs which require specialized education, experience, etc. which open up at various times. In general, Portuguese and Spanish are always good languages to have. The remuneration in the foreign field is, of course, always greater than for similar domestic work.

"We feel sure you cannot estimate too strongly the value of foreign languages in the educational requirements for the future where the world is growing smaller every day, and we are constantly coming in closer contact with foreign peoples in all areas in the business world."

That preference is given to the employee with a foreign language proficiency is pointed out by Bobby J. Schupp of the Overseas Personnel Office of the Standard Oil Co. of New Jersey:

"In most of our overseas operations, employment opportunities today are limited primarily to experienced personnel with a background related to the petroleum industry. While the majority of the requirements would be for technical personnel, there are always a few openings for persons experienced in some particular phase of refining, producing, etc. Practically all of the administrative vacancies are filled from within our company, for here, it has been demonstrated that a complete knowledge of company philosophy and policy is essential.

"While we do not require a fluency in a foreign language as a prerequisite to employment, we certainly do give consideration to this factor. We stress to all prospective employees the necessity of learning the language of the country in which he will be assigned. In some cases, language training will be provided prior to departure for the foreign location, while in others this would be taken care of after arrival. In either situation, company assistance is given.

"For an employee to be successful in overseas work, he must be conversant with the local language. Both from the social and business standpoints, he will soon discover that the ability to speak the language will put him in good stead. Much has been said relative to the adjustments that people must make when moving their home to a foreign area. Probably no one factor is more important in making this adjustment than a knowledge of the language."

OVERSEAS OPPORTUNITIES

The policy of hiring natives of the foreign country for overseas operations is the general policy of firms engaged in international business. M. F. Paul, Employment and Placement Services Manager of IBM World Trade Corporation, says:

"IBM's international operations are managed on a highly decentralized basis. Hiring decisions are made by location IBM management and the practice is to employ almost exclusively citizens of the countries in which we operate. Occasionally, Americans are hired, but their compensation is based on local economy and payable in local currency. Inquiries that are received in the United States for employment overseas are referred to the respective country personnel departments for their direct handling. The few Americans sent on temporary overseas assignment are experienced IBMers with specific knowledge of IBM's business and its policies and practices."

As indicated, however, by other personnel managers, the knowledge of a foreign language is a highly valuable asset to those sent overseas.

SALARIES

The average beginning salary for a young person entering foreign trade, who has been trained at a good business college, is $250 to $300 a week. He may be required to spend a year in special training, during which period he is provided with a car and is paid a base salary.

After an employee has completed preliminary training, he is given an overseas assignment. His salary will increase according to his responsibility. Frequently, in the case of highly competent foreign trade executives, the increases will average $2,000 a year. Bonuses, stock rights, and other fringe benefits can add appreciably to his earnings.

On the other hand, the fringe benefits must not be overrated. One foreign employment expert states that:

> "True, living allowances for certain areas are added to salaries, but grandiose expense accounts and palatial residences with large staffs of servants are myths of TV-land. A person going abroad will be provided with a sufficient allowance to live as his company expects him to live, comfortably and without ostentation. He will enjoy prospects of an adequate pension, and he and his family will have excellent health insurance coverage. The exigencies of foreign living will be taken into account . . .
>
> "As an employee's children reach high school or college age, special arrangements are usually made to assure their proper education, including provision for the children's travel to and from the family's overseas home and the United States."

QUALIFICATIONS FOR SUCCESS IN FOREIGN TRADE

Exclusive of specialized formal training in foreign trade are other qualifications which play a very important role in every individual's success. They are: intelligence, patience, tact, diplomacy, aptitude for languages, cosmopolitan viewpoint, willingness to study, attention to detail and facts, open-mindedness, willingness to put up with discomfort, adaptability, liking for foreigners, and—if married—a mate who is the type of individual who also possesses all of these characteristics.

A good qualification list for successful overseas performance has been published by the U.S. Bureau of Foreign and Domestic Commerce. It includes the following:

• Appearance: well-groomed, appropriate manners, correct speech.

• Fundamentals of international trade, economics, banking, geography, business, and international law.

• Thorough knowledge of international trade movements and practices.

• Thorough knowledge of export trade techniques.

• Thorough speaking and reading knowledge of at least one foreign language.

• Residence or travel abroad highly desirable.

• Intimate knowledge of foreign business practices.

• Ability to address public gatherings.

• Ability to write good business correspondence and reports.

• Knowledge of U.S. resources and familiarity with industrial development in this country in relation to both domestic and export trade.

To that list could be added a knowledge of America, its history, Constitution, folkways, and current events—including baseball, the World Series, movies, contemporary literature, music, and arts. An American abroad *is* America to the people with whom he associates. He must have the knowledge and skill to present and defend his valued way of life to the skeptical or misinformed.

There are failures in foreign trade careers. They are caused primarily by an inability to get along with people and to accept responsibility; a lack of self-reliance and perseverance; and the failure to identify personal goals with those of the firm and of the overall aims of American policy.

GETTING AN ASSIGNMENT OVERSEAS

Professor John Fayerweather, Associate Professor of International Business at the Graduate School of Business of Columbia University, in an article in *Export Trade* entitled "Job Hunting in the Field of International Business Operations," writes:

"Estimates of U.S. personnel employed by American companies overseas range from 25,000 to 40,000. While companies are working hard to replace Americans with local nationals, it appears that future decreases from this cause will be offset by the gains attributable to the rate of expansion of our new international investments which is running about 10% annually. Thus there are clearly numerous job openings in international operations. However, the specifications set by companies for many jobs sharply restrict the opportunities for any one individual, especially the man coming straight from college without work experience. . . .

"About 70% of U.S. overseas investments are owned by 60 large companies and some 450 companies account for about 95% of our investments. While comparable employment data are not available, undoubtedly the large companies also employ the bulk of U.S. personnel overseas.

"For the top jobs (general manager and treasurer) . . . they want mature Americans who are well versed in company operations and management skill.

". . . The men currently being sent to establish subsidiaries of the larger companies are primarily

technical specialists. . . . They have the best chances
. . . because of the dearth of suitable technical
training abroad, especially in the underdeveloped
countries."

There are several ways in which a person gets into overseas
work.

". . . a few of the larger companies hire an annual
increment of new men for their international operations . . . excluding petroleum engineers and similar
specialists probably not more than 100 men are
engaged direct from college this way each year. The
number is increasing steadily, however. . . .

"A young man goes to work as a salesman or a
production engineer for a large company with a
substantial foreign organization or a small one with
expanding interests abroad. He may have to do some
prodding and pushing to get his chance, but if he is a
good employee, an opportunity will in time open up,
perhaps in a year, more likely in two or three years."

There are about 3,000 American firms engaged in international
operations. There are jobs in international business. But the jobs
are widely dispersed and the requirements for them are often
stiff. However, if one invests careful thought and patient effort
in seeking them out, he can find a good position in one of the
most dynamic and interesting of modern management fields.

OPPORTUNITIES FOR WOMEN

In the past, the policy of international firms was to send only
men on overseas assignments, but this has changed radically. The
government and business houses are continually in need of
women to fill many responsible positions. For such jobs, a
knowledge of a foreign language is, of course, highly desirable.

In the Foreign Service of the State Department the number of women has increased rapidly. Whereas in 1973 only seven percent of the more than 3,000 Foreign Service Officers were women, the proportion is now 25 percent and is very likely to increase.

Overleaf: Airline careers provide various opportunities for multilingual

CHAPTER 5

OPPORTUNITIES IN
VARIOUS VOCATIONS

In addition to the positions where linguistic training is of prime importance, there are many other activities in which a supplemental knowledge of a foreign language is useful and highly desirable. There are also certain professional or business undertakings in which a given linguistic proficiency is basic; for example, reading ability for librarians and research workers, and speaking ability for radio broadcasters.

Below are a number of callings in which foreign languages have been found eminently useful.

AIRLINES

All American airlines flying to foreign countries require at least part of their personnel to know a foreign language. George Gardner, Educational Director of Pan American Airways, as quoted in *Vocational Opportunities for Foreign Language Students,* says:

> "As you know, Pan American World Airway routes go to all countries around the world. Employees who are sent to those other countries, of course, have to be able to speak the language of the country, and this means that we have to have employees who speak Spanish, French, German, and Portuguese and, in some cases, still other languages. Pilots generally

are qualified in a foreign language and on many routes, knowledge of a foreign language is required for stewards. In Latin America they have to be able to speak Spanish because many of their passengers speak no other language."

On most of the airlines crossing the Atlantic, stewardesses make announcements in three languages. Dr. John H. Furbay, Director, Air World Education, TWA, comments:

"Americans serving in other countries should be able to speak the languages of those countries, or suffer a great reduction in the effectiveness of their own activities. All hostesses, district managers, and others who meet the public abroad must know the language of the countries to be served. We have personnel based at 22 foreign cities along our route and approximately 100 of these employees are United States citizens, having been sent there to serve TWA. There are approximately 500 flight personnel, which includes hostesses, stewards, captains, first officers, flight engineers, and supervisors."

ADVERTISING

International advertising is a highly specialized activity. Its prime purpose, of course, is to promote the sale of American products overseas. Since the latter are sold throughout the world, all of the major and some of the lesser languages are of importance in the field of advertising.

Joseph W. Madden, Executive Vice President of National Export Advertising Service, Inc., says:

"In the important world markets today, English has become the businessman's language. Consequently, it is possible to conduct a relatively satisfactory business meeting in English.

"In order to forge lasting friendships, and therefore, more successful long-term business results, a knowledge of the particular country's language is essential. Even the simple willingness to use the local language (however badly) is welcomed—and the 'stranger' more readily becomes a friend. Fluency in the local languages, of course, greatly facilitates the whole process of establishing a mutually profitable business arrangement."

HEALTH SERVICES

More and more it is becoming evident to hospital personnel that a knowledge of certain foreign languages is urgently needed in dealing with patients, especially in metropolitan areas where there are many ethnic minorities. Doctors, nurses, technicians, and social workers find that a knowledge of Spanish or other languages is very helpful at times.

Doctors have a need for foreign languages in medical school, internship, research and clinical practice. Knowledge of a foreign tongue is essential for American students studying abroad. In 1977 over 6000 American medical students got their training in medicine at universities in Europe or Latin America. Favorite countries have recently been Italy, Belgium, and Mexico.

Specialists in medical research cannot function efficiently without a reading knowledge of Russian, German, or French.

In metropolitan areas doctors daily confront members of minority groups or recent immigrants, who cannot describe their symptoms or understand medical instructions in English. Many larger hospitals now hire bilingual personnel and provide instruction in foreign languages to their doctors, nurses, and technicians.

Jerome C. Ford of the Georgetown University School of Languages and Linguistics in Washington, D.C., comments: "The need for foreign language speakers in the medical service area, especially of Spanish, is becoming more and more acute."

Skill in a foreign language is useful to anyone engaged in health services—doctors, medical assistants, nurses, dentists and opticians. A basic knowledge of a foreign language is a necessity for anyone practicing medicine abroad, such as the American medical employees of CARE who are working overseas in the developing countries.

ARCHITECTURE

As in many other professions, a reading knowledge of several foreign languages is considered highly desirable for an architect. Professor Leopold Arnaud, Dean of the School of Architecture of Columbia University, says:

> "Most of the recognized schools of architecture consider that it is important for well-educated professionals in our field to have at least a reading knowledge of either French or German. As you probably know, the majority of our professional literature is in either English, French or German with very little written in other languages. We therefore believe that a well-educated professional should be able to read at least one other language besides English. In the case of Columbia University, we require entering students to have passed an intermediate course in either French or German."

AUTOMOBILES

Most of the large American automobile manufacturers have export divisions and maintain agencies abroad. In a number of instances they have technical and commercial arrangements with foreign companies. Ford, for instance, has its own plants in Germany and turns out a special model for that country. American cars are seen all over the world. In fact, in smaller countries where there is no automotive industry, almost sole reliance is placed on American products. Tractors from Detroit are used in Pakistan and Peru, in Norway, and Nicaragua.

The vast majority of employees in overseas operations divisions are nationals of the country in which the plant is located. A few important American representatives of the company are assigned to overseas posts. These individuals must be fluent in the foreign language. With reference to such assignments the Director of Personnel of General Motors Overseas Operations comments:

"When one of our U.S. employees is chosen for an overseas assignment, we provide language training for him and his family as part of the pre-assignment orientation offered. The amount of such training will vary with individuals, depending upon the extent of prior knowledge and their ability to absorb the training."

The International Personnel Coordinator of Chrysler Corporation states that his company requires a foreign language for candidates in their international training program. An employee without language skill assigned to an overseas position is given the opportunity of learning the language in the foreign country.

The Goodyear Tire and Rubber Company, like many other large firms, provides language training for its employees in the international field.

BANKING

In recent years many large banks have set up special departments to handle their foreign interests. It has been found necessary to maintain staffs that are linguistically competent to handle the great volume of communications. Large institutions like the Chase Manhattan Bank and Citibank work extensively in languages such as French, Spanish, German, Italian, and Russian. Translation divisions deal with the other languages in which business operations are of smaller volume. For these positions employees are preferred who have a working knowledge of several languages.

Several large banks maintain branches abroad, including the Chase National Bank and the National City Bank. In big cities, particularly in New York, there are a number of foreign banks. These, of course, have a direct need for linguistically trained personnel. Mr. Emilio Mayer of the Banca Commerciale Italiana writes:

> "Quite frequently we receive inquiries from banks or other firms engaged in foreign trade seeking office help with a knowledge of foreign languages. The inquiries pertain to receptionists, secretaries, clerks, department heads, and officers, and the languages most in demand are Spanish, Italian, French, and German.
>
> "It has been my experience that the request greatly exceeds the supply, especially if a thorough knowledge of the language is required. It seems to me that the knowledge of a foreign language gives an immediate advantage to anyone seeking a job. Furthermore, the chances for advancement are far greater, not to mention the pleasant possibility of travel abroad."

However, as was pointed out several times previously, the number of positions in certain fields is limited, and the linguistic ability must go hand in hand with some other technical skill.

This is stressed by Harmon Martin, Assistant Cashier, Personnel Department, The First National City Bank of New York, who states:

> ". . . Our firm practically never requires a language as a condition of employment except for a very few places in our Translators Department. At the present

moment this bank has less than 200 American citizens scattered among its 4,500 employees in our overseas branches."

In its *Worldwide Directory for the Corporate Client* the First National City Bank lists foreign branches, subsidiaries and affiliates in 89 countries throughout the world, ranging alphabetically from Argentina to Zaire. In 35 cities of nine different countries of South America offices and branches of the bank are maintained. This worldwide spread of operations increases the demand for many banking executives with a knowledge of foreign languages. Here in the United States, especially in metropolitan areas, many tellers are required to know Spanish.

BROADCASTING

For radio announcers the ability to speak, or at least, read a foreign language or two is a definite asset. Most announcers on the big stations do possess this ability, for they are called on every day to pronounce correctly the titles of classical musical selections, the names of operas, the names of foreign celebrities, geographical place names, and occasional quotations in a foreign language. The radio announcers on local foreign language programs in Italian, Yiddish, German, Polish, and Spanish are usually persons of foreign birth and training.

Kenneth H. Baker, Director of Research of the National Association of Broadcasters, comments, as quoted in *Vocational Opportunities for Foreign Language Students:*

"So far as we are able to discover, the only opportunity for the use of foreign languages in broadcasting would be in the actual reading of scripts in one of the many languages broadcast over standard American radio stations. A list of these languages includes:

Italian, Polish, Spanish, German, Czech-Slovak, Portuguese, Lithuanian, Hungarian, Scandinavian, Greek, French, Finnish, Yugoslav, Ukrainian, Chinese, Russian, Japanese, Roumanian, Arabic, Dutch, Albanian, Syrian, Latin, Egyptian, Armenian, and Hebrew.

"In addition to these languages, the short-wave broadcasts to other countries are also opportunities for the use of foreign languages. In this case, excellence of accent is especially desirable. . ."

David L. Doughty, Assistant to the Manager, National Association of Broadcasters, sees only a limited number of opportunities for the use of foreign languages on domestic radio and TV programs. He writes:

"Unfortunately, for the individual interested in linguistics as a career combined with broadcasting, there are very few opportunities in American radio and television. In most of the larger cities throughout the country which have good-sized foreign language populations, some stations do special language broadcasts for these groups. However, this is but a fractional segment of the jobs in American broadcasting. Insofar as foreign language students having an interest in broadcasting are concerned, I would say that their best bet would be to contact the Voice of America. . . ."

The rapidly increasing exchange of international radio programs has been commented on in connection with the use of radio and television in advertising. Of crucial importance is the use of foreign languages in military intelligence (Foreign Broadcast Intelligence Service and Monitoring Division) and for propaganda purposes ("Voice of America"). Here a high degree of skill and an impeccable pronunciation are demanded.

International broadcasting has expanded tremendously within the last few years. Arno G. Huth, Consultant to the Pan American

Broadcasting Company, writes in one of their World Wide Special Reports:

> "Today, international broadcasts, supplemented by the international exchange of television programs, originate in almost every country of the world and reach almost every nation. In the United States alone, no less than six agencies and organizations are engaged in international broadcasting. And like Great Britain and the Soviet Union, which operate the two most important international broadcasting services, Canada, Argentina, France, Italy, Poland, Czechoslovakia, Hungary, Indonesia, India, Pakistan, Australia, and many others are broadcasting day and night in many different languages.

> "International broadcasting offers great potentialities for worldwide advertising. There are, in various areas of the world, private as well as official stations which accept foreign-sponsored programs and which, although broadcasting mainly in the national language, are prepared to carry foreign-language programs destined to minority groups or to listeners in adjacent countries."

HOTEL SERVICE

With the devaluation of the dollar and increased prosperity in a number of foreign countries, travel in the United States has grown considerably; in 1972, over three million foreign visitors arrived here. Although great pains have been taken to provide comfortable hotel accommodations and travel facilities, the language barrier still remains a problem. Many foreign visitors suffer more than a little inconvenience because most Americans can converse in no language other than English.

Some efforts have been made to remedy this fault by employing multilingual travel personnel. The United States Travel Service maintains a Multilingual Port Receptionist Program in which over 70 young people with foreign language competence are active. "Travel Phone USA" provides a nationwide toll-free telephone interpreter service in Spanish, French, German, and Japanese. These services are sure to expand and it has been predicted that jobs in the tourist business will double within the next few years.

The United States Travel Service has stressed the importance of language equipment; its language certification program certifies hotels with multilingual personnel. There are about 250 multilingual hotels whose staffs speak French, German, Spanish, and Japanese. In addition there are over a thousand other establishments with bilingual personnel. Most of the larger metropolitan hotels have waiters and chambermaids of foreign origin who can function as interpreters when needed. The Hotel Hilton in New York, for example, has employees speaking 36 different languages.

The personnel director of the Waldorf-Astoria Hotel in New York writes:

> "We have a large number of guests from abroad, and to take care of the situation where languages are involved, we have a Foreign Department, the head of which speaks approximately eight languages fluently. We also have in that department an assistant who speaks Spanish and Portuguese fluently and several other employees, such as stenographers, typists, etc., who are linguists. I think that the knowledge of a foreign language, or several languages, is an aid in securing employment in any large hotel where they would be likely to have clientele from abroad."

C. L. O'Connor, Manager of the Hotel Wellington, New York, states:

> "We do have a need for hotel personnel who speak the major European languages. At the present time

we have, in our Front Office Department, employees who speak the following languages: French, Spanish, and German.

"In various other departments of the hotel we have employees whom we occasionally call upon for translation or interpretations of Swedish or Italian.

"We probably use our Spanish interpreter more than any of the others."

INTERNATIONAL RELATIONS

The number of cultural, commercial, and relief associations interested in foreign relations is constantly increasing. On their staffs they need translators, librarians, research workers, representatives, and receptionists. The Institute of International Education has about 15 persons equipped with foreign languages. The latter are French, German, Spanish, and Portuguese.

On the research staff of the Foreign Policy Association there are a number of persons who know at least one foreign language.

The wide expansion of the field of international relations and the large number of Americans participating in it are stressed in a World Wide Special Report of the Pan American Broadcasting Company:

"Technical assistance operations are undertaken in almost every part of the world. Since the inception of the program (Expanded Program of Technical Assistance of the U.N.), some 1,600 experts in a wide variety of fields, drawn from 61 different nations, have been employed by the United Nations and its specialized agencies; of these, 956 were in the field, working in underdeveloped countries and territories, at the requests of the governments directly concerned. They surveyed local conditions, provided advice, demonstrated new techniques, set up schools and training centers, and conducted seminars and vocational courses.

Simultaneously, under various scholarship and fellow-
ship programs, hundreds of civil servants, technicians,
and students from underdeveloped countries are en-
abled to study abroad modern techniques of public
administration, health and welfare services, and agricultural and industrial production."

JOURNALISM

In considering journalism and foreign languages, one thinks of
two large areas: the foreign language press of the United States
and the foreign departments of English-language newspapers. The
former is taken care of largely by natives but, in the second, there
are attractive positions for qualified Americans. There is the local
staff consisting of newsmen, translators, and the foreign corres-
pondents in various parts of the world. The language facility required is of a high order. L. B. Mickel of the United Press Association comments:

"The United Press application for employment
asks: 'What languages other than English do you
speak and write *fluently?*' We are not interested in
those who reply: 'Had four years of German' or 'can
read Spanish,' etc.

"For instance, we expect an employee on our
Paris staff to be able to understand French from an
excited native trying to send in a story on the phone.
If you can handle news on the phone in a foreign
language, you have to be good.

"If a man says he can speak Russian, we expect
him to understand a Russian broadcast and be able to
report it accurately."

H. W. Burch, of the United Press Association, New York,
writes:

"Command of at least one foreign language long has been almost a necessity in the world press association field for any aspiring journalist, since so great a part of news gathering and distribution passes beyond local or national boundaries. The importance, therefore, of foreign language study for anyone hoping to enter world journalism is plain.

"The expansion of world communications also has brought new emphasis to the need for foreign language study. This applies in many ways: the great increase in world travel has brought many more foreign students and journalists into contact with each other, forcing them to increase their language facility; a vast increase in the volume of news which can be delivered to remote points by modern radio channels has brought all public information media into closer, speedier contact; the pressures of hot and cold wars, and the dislocations accompanying them have forced interchanges between populations, and accompanying exchange of language habits.

"As distribution of news abroad increases with the aid of new radio and telegraphic communications devices, demand increases for editorial workers capable of handling one or more languages. The United Press now transmits its entire news report to Latin America in Spanish, with a full translation-editorial staff employed in New York solely for the purpose of writing the service in Spanish.

"It also is worth noting that as the United States has assumed leadership in so many fields of world activity, New York and Washington have become the headquarters for many offices and directive bureaus employing translators, interviewers, commentators, and executives with a command of languages.

"There are, in fact, so many visible opportunities for the bilingual or trilingual person that no persuasion should be needed for the aspiring student or adult to perfect himself in a foreign language."

LIBRARIAN

Knowledge of a foreign language is an important asset to a librarian, especially in the cataloging and reference departments.

Helen R. Sattley, Director, School Library Service, New York, says:

> "There are indeed many opportunities open in the library field for young people who are adequately trained in one or more foreign languages. All of our library schools require that students present a background in foreign language study for admittance.
>
> "Concerning the opportunities for work in library fields for those with a foreign language background, there is much to be said at the present time. For example, all of our large city libraries have foreign book collections. Some of these cities have special branches which concentrate on specific foreign language books. Also, large and important technical and science libraries, and departments of science and technology in large libraries need librarians who can read the technical German and French reference books, journals, and magazines. This field is an expanding one at the present time and there is a need for many young men and women who are specifically trained for these positions.
>
> "There have been openings in library service outside of the United States; for instance, the information libraries of the United States Department of State have been developed in many important cities throughout the world. It is usual in these libraries for the librarian to meet a foreign language requirement for the country in which the library is located.
>
> "There are also permanent libraries in foreign countries, such as the American Library in Paris and the Benjamin Franklin Library in Mexico City.

Librarians in these need to have excellent backgrounds in French and Spanish, respectively. There are at the present time and will be in the future, many opportunities for exchange positions among American librarians and those of other countries. A foreign language background will be a necessary requirement. . . ."

In view of these needs, library schools generally require at least a reading knowledge of a foreign language. Anita M. Hostetter, Secretary, Board of Education for Librarianship, American Library Association, says:

"Even library schools which require a foreign language point out that all fields of library work do not require a reading knowledge of foreign languages. This information is needed in scholarly and scientific library service, in bibliographic work, cataloging of large collections or specialized reference work. If a knowledge of foreign language is essential for library work of a given type, the librarian should usually have more competence than it is possible to gain through two years of study at the college level.

"The modern languages which have proved most generally useful in library service are German, French, and, in some geographic locations, Spanish. Other languages such as Italian, the Slavonic languages, and others are needed in some highly specialized positions. A knowledge of foreign languages is becoming of increasing importance to young American librarians as opportunities for library service abroad develop. The United States Information Libraries operated by the State Department in many countries generally require or prefer a speaking and writing knowledge of the language of the country."

Faye Simkin, Executive Officer of the New York Public Library, writes:

> "The Research Libraries have three major language divisions—the Jewish, Oriental, and Slavonic Divisions. In addition, the General Research and Humanities Division houses material in most other foreign languages as do our subject divisions. Some 3,000 languages are represented in the collections by language. Among current acquisitions, 50 percent have been ordered in a language other than English.
>
> "A knowledge of foreign languages is, of course, a great asset in working in the Research Libraries. However, it is equally as important to have subject skills and to possess the ability to work well in the area of human relationships, both with fellow staff members and the general public."

The New York Public Library, in addition to its vast central reference collection, maintains circulating collections in branch libraries in 22 foreign languages. These are: Chinese, Croatian, Czech, Danish, Dutch, Finnish, French (9 branches), German (8), Greek, Hebrew (3), Hungarian (3), Italian (5), Lithuanian, Norwegian, Polish, Portuguese, Russian, Slovak, Spanish (4), Swedish, Ukrainian, Yiddish (4).

MOTION PICTURES

There are a number of sections of the motion picture industry in which a knowledge of foreign languages is useful. William Zimmerman, Director, Narrated & Titled Films Department of Metro-Goldwyn-Mayer, writes:

> "We employ several young people who have a knowledge of one or more foreign languages. Their

knowledge of these languages was a prerequisite of their employment.

"The main languages used in this department (the department in this company which has the greatest use for bilingual or multilingual personnel) are Spanish, French, and Portuguese (for Brazil), although we do work in many other languages."

Several years ago John T. Madden, Personnel Director of the same concern, wrote:

"We employ persons who are both bilingual and multilingual in the production of films for foreign distribution. As a rule, however, these persons were born in the foreign countries or have a very large background of skill and experience in the language. We also employ translators in the several languages, such as French, German, Spanish, and occasionally other languages."

MUSEUM WORK

As in every field of research, in museum work there is need for a knowledge of foreign languages. John R. Saunders, Chairman of the Department of Public Instruction of the American Museum of Natural History, New York, says:

"I should say that in any large museum, whether it be devoted to art, science or history, a command of one or more foreign languages would be a definite asset to a staff member. Most museums cannot afford to employ translators regularly. They usually depend upon the linguistic ability of their regular staff. Most of our staff who are concerned with research have at least a reading knowledge of French and German. Several are adept in Spanish. Those who do their field work in Mexico, Central America, and South America find it necessary to learn to speak and understand Spanish. When a translation problem comes up at the Museum, resources are pooled, and since we make a language ability survey every so often, there is usually someone on hand who can assist in the matter."

PUBLISHING

There are some 40 important publishers of foreign language books in the United States. Dr. Vincenzo Cioffari, formerly the Modern Language Editor of D. C. Heath & Company, one of the oldest and largest firms in this field, comments:

"Whereas a few years ago the publishing industry dealt almost exclusively with printed textbooks, now it has to deal with complete programs which include tapes, records, charts, television courses, programmed courses, and other materials. Consequently there has been an increase not only in the actual editorial staffs, but in supplementary staffs which deal with laboratories, audio-visual materials, television programs, etc.

"On the whole, publishing houses have an editorial staff composed of people who are quite familiar with two, three or four modern foreign languages. These staffs are responsible for the correctness of the foreign language that gets into print. When necessary, these staffs are expanded by the use of part-time, trained editors who work at home.

"In addition to the actual editorial staff, there is a staff of proofreaders maintained by the press rather than the publisher. There is a staff of trained technicians maintained by recording studios dealing with tapes, records or television programs. All of these people must be familiar with foreign languages; the more languages they have at their command, the more valuable they are.

"In the art, manufacturing, and accounting departments, it certainly helps to be able to understand titles and contents of books which pass through. People who work in the publicity department can manage to get along without foreign languages, but their work is far more efficient if they have a knowledge of them. In fact, in all phases of work, the publisher of foreign language programs finds knowledge of several foreign languages a distinct and valuable asset."

SECRETARY

The most attractive position in business for a beginner, and possibly the easiest one to qualify for, is that of bilingual stenographer or secretary. These jobs are quite numerous. Of the 477 advertisements requiring a foreign language competency in five Sunday editions of *The New York Times,* no fewer than 350 called for an office assistant. These positions are on different levels, depending upon the size and character of the business and on the preparation of the applicant.

Although this type of job is usually associated with typing and stenography—the basic skills of the secretary—the duties may go far beyond that. The office assistant may be a typist, a stenographer, a receptionist, a file clerk or may be the chief executive's confidential secretary and aid. The latter position of trust and importance is, of course, attained only after years of faithful service and experience.

Average distribution of languages in want-ads for bilingual personnel in the *New York Times* for five successive Sundays:

Spanish	32
French	30
German	16
Italian	2
Other	3

SOCIAL WORK

In metropolitan areas, most social workers deal practically every day with members of minority groups, and without some knowledge of a foreign language, they cannot work effectively. This is evident in the want-ads for social workers, most of which now ask for competency in Spanish. Some of the larger social service agencies, like Cancer Care and Travelers Air International Social Service of America, now require their workers to have a knowledge of Spanish; Italian, Chinese, and modern Greek also are useful, depending upon the ethnic group with which the social worker is dealing.

Other organizations like the Salvation Army, the Volunteers of America, the Red Cross, and the Y.M.C.A. also have urged some of their employees to develop competence in a foreign language for use in their social-service work.

Professor Arthur Dunham of the School of Social Work of the University of Michigan says:

"In at least a minority of positions in social work, knowledge of certain foreign languages would be of real practical value. These positions would include such jobs as the following: (1) social work in foreign countries; (2) social work with certain American agencies working primarily with the foreign born, such as the International Institutes, organizations working with displaced persons; (3) social work in certain districts of larger cities."

FOREIGN MISSIONARIES

The missionary field is one in which tens of thousands of persons of all nations are engaged. It covers the entire globe and embraces all languages. A knowledge of a foreign language is indispensable to a missionary if he wants to be effective. He must not only be able to converse in the tongue of the native but is often called upon to translate technical matter and poetry (hymns) into the foreign language.

In fact, in a number of instances, it was the missionary who gave the language its written form. Bishop Cyril gave the Russians their alphabet; Wulfilas translated the Bible into Gothic and invented the script. In South America, Spanish missionaries and priests constructed grammars and recorded the language of the natives, as in the case of Quechua, the language of the Incas.

The total number of American foreign missionaries throughout the world in 1973 was 41,745, of which 34,057 were Protestant missionaries and 7,691 Catholic missionaries.

According to a 1973 survey, the following countries within Asia and Africa received the most North American Protestant missionaries, that is, from the United States and Canada. Of the total of 34,057, only 1,013 came from Canada.

The Protestant distribution was:

Asia		Africa	
Japan	1,931	Zaire	1,052
India	1,247	Nigeria	1,032
Philippines	1,187	Kenya	645
Indonesia	756	Ethiopia	598
Taiwan	567	South Africa	528
Korea	474		

The Catholic distribution:

Asia		Africa	
Japan	368	Zaire	26
India	191	Nigeria	37
Philippines	585	Kenya	146
Indonesia	52	Ethiopia	35
Taiwan	218	South Africa	46
Korea	185		

TRANSLATORS

In its broadest sense, as applied to language, translation is the act or process of expressing an idea or message in some target language other than the source language in which it is given to the translator. Translation of the spoken language is called "interpretation" and the term "translation" is reserved primarily for written or printed material. The distinction is important, because the two activities make use of quite different linguistic skills. Translators need have little facility in the spoken language since their work does not require it. Consequently they tend to avoid acting as interpreters, although some are called upon for that purpose occasionally.

There is a wide demand for translators in business, in various research organizations, and in government service. The New York City Classified Telephone Directory lists over sixty translation bureaus, chiefly of a commercial nature.

Those who go into this field must be prepared to deal with all kinds of scientific, technical, commercial, and legal material. Many translators work free-lance. The director of the Engineering Societies Library says:

"We do not employ full-time translators, but use part-time help. Most of our translation is from German to English or from French to English, but during the past year we have translated Italian, Japanese, Hungarian, Russian, Spanish and probably other languages. The rate of payment depends on the difficulty of the work and the language."

The three main categories of materials that are most frequently translated are commercial, literary, and technical. The first category includes letters, contracts, and advertisements; the second consists of novels, poems, and historical articles. The technical category comprises the various sciences and engineering.

The translator must be familiar not only with both languages but should also have some knowledge of the subject covered in the text. This frequently entails extensive research and the use of special technical dictionaries.

A translation can be considered successful only if it achieves its purpose. A good literary translation should convey the emotional and artistic as well as the informational content of the original. The language should be completely normal and natural, so that the reader is almost unaware that he or she is dealing with a translation.

To qualify as an efficient translator, the student should have a well-rounded college education. In addition to the language course, the aspirant should cover many special areas such as science, history, law, economics, and literature.

The constant growth in the number of U.S. patents issued to residents of other countries has created an increasing need for technical translators. The expansion of American business all over the world has raised the demand for translators of correspondence, advertising, and technical matter. Managers of some translation bureaus report an increase of up to 300 percent over the past three or four years.

A growing number of American industries maintain language staffs of one or more translators. Such are Rockwell International, Otis Engineering, Honeywell, Kodak, etc. Salaries are somewhat higher than those offered by international agencies, but the translator in private industry is usually required to have competence in a number of languages—five or more—and to act as escort interpreter for visitors and telephone calls.

The number of positions in which translating alone is required are not very numerous. In business the practice is to hire someone proficient in one or more languages and who also possesses a technical skill such as banking, marketing, foreign trade, etc.

Translators and interpreters are employed in different departments of the federal government and the United Nations. There are also positions available in publishing houses and firms doing business with foreign countries.

Salaries depend not only on linguistic proficiency but also on the degree of technical skill in some other area. They range from $10,500 to $25,000 a year. At the United Nations the beginning salary is $18,000. In the federal government translators with a B.A. degree are given GS-5 or GS-7 ratings (depending on college grades). In 1979 annual earnings in these grades were $10,507 for GS-5 and $13,014 for GS-7.

Although there are many staff translators, the majority are free-lance and work as they are needed. Average fees charged by self-employed translators range from $40 to $80 per thousand words.

The largest single producer of translations among the government agencies is the Joint Publications Research Service, an agency of the Central Intelligence Agency. Most of the translating is done by free-lance translators instead of private translation services. The bulk of JPRS translation work is from Soviet and East European publications.

Translation is a very important and interesting activity. The daily production will vary with the difficulty of the text. Most translators are expected to complete between 2,000 and 4,000 words per day of finished typed translations, but some experienced translators, who dictate, are capable of translating more than 20,000 words per day.

A list of schools offering training for translators and interpreters is available from the American Translators Association, PO Box 129, Croton-on-Hudson, N. Y., 10520. For approximately $3.50 the list and "Guidelines for Translator Programs" can be obtained. Valuable information may also be secured from the Language Service Division, U.S. Department of State, Washington, D. C., 20520.

TRAVEL AND TOURISM

Strangely enough, the need for a foreign language background is not as urgent in the travel agency field as one might expect.

W. F. McGrath, Executive Vice President of the American Society of Travel Agents, writes:

> "There is no way of knowing to what extent the use of foreign languages would be used in the travel field, as this would depend on the type of business only. By and large, travel agents in this country utilize the services of corresponding firms in foreign countries for most services and do not have to be linguists. In addition, the use of the English language is universal in the travel industry."

However, in all metropolitan areas there are travel agents who do employ foreign languages in dealing with their clients of foreign birth.

The Personnel Director of the American Express Company expresses an opinion similar to that of Mr. McGrath:

"American Express, insofar as the United States is concerned, has relatively little need for staff who are fluent in foreign languages, since they are dealing primarily with an American public and with members of staff of our foreign public offices who almost invariably speak English in addition to their native tongue. We do, as a matter of fact, employ a very limited number of young executive trainees in the United States for foreign service, and although we do not insist upon it, ability in foreign languages is a decided asset, a point strongly in their favor when considered for employment and of great advantage to them individually in most of our locations overseas."

Tour guides at United Nations headquarters in New York City. Tours can be conducted in a total of 37 languages.

Photo: United Nations / M. Grant.

On the actual tour or trip, however, knowledge of a foreign language is essential. George H. Copeland, in his *Planning a Cruise,* says:

> "Once the cruise is under way, it is the job of the staff, particularly of the hostesses, to see that all the careful plans come off with an effect of spontaneity. ... In addition to being something of an amateur psychologist, a hostess must be able to speak more than one language—on the Home Lines, a hostess must have a knowledge of at least four."

In 1975 almost 16,000,000 tourists visited the United States and spent $4,875,000,000. They came mainly from Canada, Mexico, Japan, the United Kingdom, and West Germany.

Overleaf: Interpreters aid members of the State Department, the Senate Foreign Relations Committee, and members of Chinese Vice Premier Deng Xiaoping's party at a reception in the Senate Rotunda. (Photo: Office of Senate Howard H. Baker.)

CHAPTER 6

OPPORTUNITIES IN GOVERNMENT POSITIONS

The United States government is the largest employer in the country, with 2½ million employees. It is also the largest employer of persons equipped with foreign language skills. Most federal employees occupying such positions are employed as translators and bilingual stenographers.

CIVIL SERVICE

In the broad sense of the word, civil servants conduct the various activities of local, state, and federal government offices. Almost one out of every six Americans is a civil servant, and almost every type of work carried on in private business and industry is also found in government service. The range of Civil Service jobs is wide, including carpenters, plumbers, auto mechanics, policemen, doctors, and judges.

In many government activities, an employee may be called upon to make use of a foreign language. This is particularly true in large metropolitan areas like New York, Philadelphia, Chicago, and San Francisco, where there are large concentrations of foreign-born and minority groups. Within recent years, the need for a knowledge of Spanish has become so urgent that special courses have been arranged for policemen, doctors, nurses, and social workers.

Formerly, special civil service examinations were scheduled for the positions of translator and bilingual stenographer. This has been changed, and at present, the applicant is to apply directly to the agency for which he expects to work. Complete job information and forms may be obtained at any one of the Federal Job Information Centers which are found in all large cities.

DEPARTMENT OF STATE

Charles W. Curtis, Chief, Recruitment Operations Branch, Division of Personnel, Department of State, writes:

"We are in complete agreement that knowledge of foreign languages is becoming of greater importance to Americans, especially in the international activities of our governemnt.

"In the Department of State, there are a number of positions which require foreign language facility. A high degree of language proficiency is a basic requirement for such positions as Information Officer, Cultural Affairs Officer, and Public Affairs Officer in the Information Program in Europe and Latin America. It is also desirable for such positions in the Near and Middle East.

"However, other positions in the Department require a higher degree of language proficiency than is ordinarily acquired by traditional academic language training. For example, the Linguistic Scientist employed in our Foreign Service Institute must have a degree in Linguistic Science from an American university, plus teaching experience and professional competence in from one to three languages. The higher salaried positions require a Ph.D. in Linguistic Science in addition to considerable teaching proficiency in at least three languages.

"Our Division of Language Service employs

Language Typists, Translators, Reviewers, and Interpreters, in approximately the same salary range. Most of the people occupying the positions now have had extensive foreign residence in addition to a thorough academic training. A minimum of two languages is necessary and the majority of these employees handle four or more. Applicants must have an M.A. or Ph.D. in languages, or an equivalent combination of academic training and pertinent work experience. In either case, without actual work or school experience in a foreign country, applicants generally are unable to satisfactorily pass the qualifying examination given by the Division of Language Services here in Washington. In the Interpreter-Reviewer-Translator category, we mainly use French, Spanish, Portuguese, and some German, Italian and Russian. . . ."

A government bulletin further describes translating jobs in the Department of State as follows:

"The Division of Language Services is responsible for all official translating and interpreting services for the Department of State. This includes (a) translation from foreign languages into English and from English into foreign languages; (b) providing interpreting, translating, and related stenographic services for international conferences; (c) reviewing draft treaties before signature to assure substantive conformity between the English and foreign-language texts; and (d) providing escort interpreters for the international educational exchange program and similar programs.

"Translators are, as a general rule, asked to translate into their native language. A translator must, therefore, be able to write his native language with a high degree of stylistic skill and have an expert knowledge of the language or languages from which the translations are made. Most translator positions in the Department are for translation into English. Because of the wide range of subject matter involved, the translator must have a very good educational background and broad experience.

"Translators into English are usually required to have a fluent knowledge of at least two foreign languages. Translators into foreign languages are required to translate from English into only one language. However, they must be able to write that language with all the skill of a professional writer in the areas where the language is spoken, since practically all such translations are intended for distribution abroad.

"The Department's interpreters are called upon to interpret from English into one or more foreign languages or from one or more foreign languages into English at official talks, conferences or during escort assignments. Both the simultaneous and consecutive systems of interpretation are used. The interpreter must be exceptionally fluent in the languages into which he interprets, and his speech must be free of any objectionable accent. Like the translator, the interpreter should have a good general educational background, supplemented, if possible, by practical experience in several fields, since he may be called upon to handle topics in widely divergent fields."

FOREIGN SERVICE

One of the most attractive jobs in the Department of State for a college graduate with skill in a foreign language and a desire to travel is that of a Foreign Service officer.

The following information is taken from a bulletin issued by the State Department with reference to openings:

The Department of State is responsible for conducting relations with foreign nations and international organizations; for protecting and advancing political, economic, and other interests of the United States overseas, and for rendering a variety of services to individual Americans abroad. Much of this work is carried out by Foreign Service officers, who, when abroad, serve as diplomatic and consular officers and who, when in Washington, fill most of the more responsible positions in the State Department.

All Foreign Service officers are expected to be well-informed regarding foreign and domestic affairs; be knowledgeable about U.S. government, history, and culture; and be able to speak and write effectively. All officers should be interested in people and have the ability to move easily in business, government, and professional circles.

Competitive examinations are held periodically for appointments as Foreign Service officers or information officers of the U.S. Information Agency (USIA). The majority of the candidates usually are college graduates, but men and women with professional and vocational experience outside college also are encouraged to take the examination. Professional backgrounds are especially sought by USIA for its junior officer positions which increasingly require relevant experience in communications media, cross-cultural communications, American civilization, foreign languages and literature, area studies, and other fields related to the functions of information and cultural affairs officers.

Since the Foreign Service officially represents the United States to other nations, the Department of State and USIA are particularly interested in recruiting increased numbers of members of minority groups, including women. As Equal Employment Opportunity employers, both the Department of State and USIA adhere to the policy of providing employment opportunities to everyone regardless of race, sex, marital status, religion or ethnic background.

Upon completion of the examination and selection process, successful candidates are appointed by the President, by and with the consent of the Senate. Usually officers can expect to serve two of their first three tours abroad. A normal tour lasts two years, but may be longer or shorter depending upon conditions at the post and the needs of the Service. Officers are expected to be available for worldwide service, as are their families.

Depending on their qualifications, successful candidates are appointed at Class 8 ($15,423 to $17,479) or Class 7 ($13,925 to $15,781). New officers serve in probationary status until their first promotion. The promotion ladder numerically culminates at a present salary level of $60,657. While officers are abroad, their salaries may be supplemented by quarters allowances, cost-of-living allowances, hardship post differentials, and educational allowances for children, depending on local conditions.

Applicants must indicate whether they wish to be examined for service in one of four functional specializations in the Department of State (administrative, consular, economic/commercial or political) or in the information/cultural specialty leading to appointment with the U.S. Information Agency.

ELIGIBILITY REQUIREMENTS

Applicants must be at least 21 years of age and citizens of the United States by the date of the written examination. (However, a person 20 years of age as of that date may be examined if the junior year of college has been successfully completed.) There is no upper age limit other than the requirement that a newly appointed officer be able to serve at least one complete tour abroad before reaching the mandatory retirement age of 60 years.

If a candidate is married to a non-U.S. citizen, the spouse must be naturalized before the candidate can be appointed as a Foreign Service officer.

Applications to take the Foreign Service officer examination for service with the U.S. Information Agency or the Department of State should be sent to the Board of Examiners for the Foreign

Service (USIA), P.O. Box 9317, Rosslyn Station, Arlington, Virginia 22209.

EDUCATIONAL PREPARATION

There are no specific educational requirements for appointment to the Foreign Service. However, the written and oral examinations are difficult, and a broad general knowledge is needed to pass them. Moreover, to be an effective representative of the United States abroad, an officer must possess a sound knowledge of the history, government, and culture of the U.S. people; be familiar with foreign and domestic affairs, and be informed regarding current events. Ability to write and speak effectively also is essential.

The best preparation for a Foreign Service career is a good general education, combined with school or practical work experience. Such an education may be obtained at any good undergraduate, graduate or professional school and might include courses in history, government, economics, literature, and a foreign language. These courses should be supplemented by selective reading of books, newspapers, and journals concerned with current events and foreign affairs.

While language instruction and other training are provided at government expense at the State Department's Foreign Service Institute after appointment, no training, financial aid or scholarships of any kind are provided beforehand for students and others wishing to prepare themselves for careers in the Foreign Service.

LANGUAGE REQUIREMENT

Knowledge of a foreign language is not a requirement for appointment to the Foreign Service. After appointment, however, officers are expected to acquire an acceptable level of proficiency in at least one foreign language, and junior officers are limited to no more than one promotion until they do so. New officers are given language tests after they begin duty. Those who pass a speaking and reading test in one of forty or more foreign languages end their language probation and in some instances become eligible to receive a higher salary in their officer class. Full-time language training is provided at government expense as necessary.

JOBS FOR WOMEN

The following information is taken from a special circular of the Department of State entitled: *The Foreign Service Officer Corps as a Career for Women: Commonly Asked Questions:*

As of December 31, 1973, about seven percent or 239 of the 3,303 Foreign Service officers were women. Special efforts have been made to encourage women to take the examination. Over 25 percent of the officers appointed between August 1973 and March 1974 were women.

Marital status is not considered, and a woman receives the same benefits for her family as does a man. A husband and children may accompany the female officer abroad as do the dependents of a male officer. A spouse may work for an employer other than the U.S. government.

There are over 30 working couples serving in posts abroad. Every effort is made to assign both members to the same post. Women may take leave for maternity purposes and resume their careers. Female officers have the same worldwide assignment possibilities as male officers, and they may serve in any position for which they are qualified in any part of the world.

The mandatory retirement age is 60. In practice, this means that no one over the age of 57 would be appointed. The Foreign

Service is particularly interested in attracting women who have some prior professional experience in addition to those who have recently completed their formal education.

U.S. INFORMATION AGENCY

From a brochure issued by the United States Information Agency the following information is taken:

The USIA operates with press, radio, film, television, libraries, exhibits, the arts, and personal contact with its officers. Over 1,250 Agency officers are employed at 219 posts in 99 countries. The officers are aided by some 6,000 trained assistants who operate the libraries, show the films, translate the texts, and display the exhibits.

The full range of editorial techniques is employed for the coverage of current events. The Agency publishes for foreign language publications in Russian, Polish, Spanish, and Arabic. USIA posts overseas produce 69 other magazines in 25 languages and 20 newspapers.

The Agency operates 176 libraries, 85 reading rooms, and supports 128 binational centers abroad. These facilities attract some 30 million visitors annually. The libraries contain over 2,500,000 books.

International Broadcasting is also a function of the Information Agency. Positions are filled from lists of individuals who have qualified by passing civil service examinations given under the direction of the Board of U.S. Civil Service Examiners, U.S. Information Agency, Washington, D.C. 20415. Examinations cover one or more of 86 named foreign languages.

Each year a highly select group of young people begin careers in international broadcasting. They are given a year's intensive training to prepare them to become skilled radio professionals.

Requirements for the career intern program include a college degree or equivalent in communications, radio-T.V., broadcasting, journalism, foreign affairs, government and foreign languages. In general the special skills which are helpful for careers with the Voice of America include the ability to speak and write a foreign language fluently, the possession of a voice suitable for radio broadcasting, and experience in radio writing, editing, or producing.

The U.S. Civil Service Commission gives the following figures for linguists in the Federal Government. A total of 321 persons are employed as translators and interpreters in the U.S. and in overseas locations. Most of these are in the Department of the Army, the Air Force, the Department of State, in the Library of Congress, and in the Department of Justice. Some 150 are in foreign language broadcasting and 150 are in the United States Information Agency.

THE VOICE OF AMERICA

An extremely interesting field in which there are thousands of positions is the Voice of America (VOA), maintained by the U.S. Information Agency in Washington.

James Keogh, Director, U.S.I.A., gives the following description of the operations of the international broadcasts in a folder entitled *Facts About VOA:*

The Voice of America is the global network of the U.S. Information Agency which seeks to promote understanding abroad for the United States, its people, culture and policies. VOA broadcasts support these efforts through objective and comprehensive news reports and through feature programs projecting a balanced and in-depth picture of American society, thought, institutions, arts, and music. As an official radio, VOA strives to present the policies of the United States clearly and effectively, including responsible opinion and comment on these policies.

Programs:

Languages—35 languages regularly scheduled; other languages specially programmed.

Direct Broadcasts—776 hours per week (compared with 1,968 by USSR; 1,293, People's Republic of China; 1,089, Arab Republic of Egypt; 782, Federal Republic of Germany; 729, United Kingdom)

Indirect Broadcasts—4,000 local radio stations in other countries also broadcast programs prepared by VOA and/or USIA posts abroad. VOA further supports USIA overseas information and cultural programs with materials taped and written.

Audience:

More than 50 million adults over the age of 14 listen to VOA direct broadcasts in a given week.

Facilities:

Studios—23 in Washington, D.C.; 3 in New York City; 1 in Miami; 1 in Los Angeles; 1 in Chicago.

Master Control—Located in Washington, D.C.

Domestic Transmitters—41, located in Bethany, Ohio; Delano and Dixon, California; Marathon, Florida; Greenville, North Carolina.

Overseas Transmitters—72, located in Sri Lanka, the Philippines, Morocco, Liberia, England, Federal Republic of Germany, Okinawa, Greece, and Thailand.

Power—Total, all in 113 transmitters—22,300,000 watts.

Personnel:

2,259 authorized positions (1,346 in the United States and 913, including foreign nationals, abroad.)

Budget:

$56,000,000 (operating budget, fiscal year 1975)

The programs of VOA are prepared and broadcast by native speakers or by Americans with near-native competency, usually, persons who were brought up bilingually or have lived in the foreign country. In addition to linguistic facility, a thorough area knowledge is required.

In addition to the VOA broadcasts there is the radio monitoring service. This is engaged in obtaining information from foreign radio broadcasts. The language monitor is required to listen directly to foreign broadcasts and to provide comprehensive summaries of significant portions of the broadcasts. These summaries are made available to other government agencies.

Since the broadcasts monitored are in foreign tongues spoken by natives in the foreign country, a monitor must have an almost native degree of fluency. He must also possess the ability to translate into correct, fluent English. In order to do this with facility, the monitor must also possess a good knowledge of current political and economic conditions in the foreign country. Since the speech of the foreign speaker is usually rapid, the monitor must have a keen auditory sense.

The major languages involved are French, Spanish, German, Russian, Italian, and Chinese.

IMMIGRATION AND NATURALIZATION SERVICE

The New York District of the Immigration and Naturalization Service maintains a staff of interpreters who do the interpreting and translating in connection with immigration matters. The positions are under the Civil Service and are filled in accordance with current laws and regulations.

Abraham Wassner, the Supervising Director of the Interpreter Section of the U.S. Immigration Service, has this to say about his department:

"The staff consists of regular, permanently appointed interpreters and of interim interpreters. Of
the former there are ten in the New York office. A
much larger number of part-time interpreters is hired
on a per diem basis. They receive $36.50 for a daily
assignment, which may last only two hours. The
regular interpreters are on a standard annual wage
scale, according to their grade.

"The interpreting service is not confined to the
New York office; it extends to many parts of the
world. Offices are maintained in Paris, Frankfurt,
Athens, the Virgin Islands, and Montreal. Service is
also provided throughout the United States by telephone, since the interpreter 'is heard but need not be
seen.' Stations are maintained in New Orleans, San
Francisco, and other cities of the West.

"Twenty-nine principal languages are used, but a
great many rare and exotic languages, as well as
dialects and even jargon, are called for. The very
names of some of these are now generally familiar, as
for instance, Khler (Cambodia), Twi (Gambia), and
Gujarati (India). The little known languages and
dialects, of which almost a hundred are listed, are the
ones for which it is difficult to find competent interpreters. Within a year about a hundred extra personnel are hired for such languages. As far as the
standard, major languages are concerned there is no
difficulty at all; plenty of capable linguists are available. After selecting the interim interpreters, the
Director trains them and gives them their assignments."

This staff of interpreters is, of course, highly trained and well
experienced. All of them speak a number of languages. In addition, many of the Immigrant Inspectors and Investigators have
competence in one or more of the commoner languages. This is
definitely an asset in dealing with people coming from so many

foreign countries. Officers in these categories have been promoted to the highest ranks of the service, and, as an administrative assistant says, although it cannot be said that their promotion was because of a language ability, certainly it was not a hindrance.

DEFENSE

Foreign languages play an important role in the U.S. Department of Defense which includes the Army, Navy, Air Force, and Marine Corps. The National Security Agency is also part of the Department of Defense. The foreign operations by the various branches require the services of many individuals with foreign language skills. To make these available, special language schools have been established.

The West Coast Branch of the Defense Language Institute of the Army teaches 25 languages to military personnel. Native speakers are preferred as instructors but a limited number of American-born instructors are also hired. The positions are at GS-7 level. The minimum language requirement is described as follows:

"The applicant must have speaking proficiency of the target language equivalent to that of an educated native speaker, free from undesirable accents or defects. He must have the ability to write the language with accurate sentence structure and proper expression of ideas, and possess the ability of stylistic discrimination."

The Acting Chief of the Recruitment and Examining Section, Staff Civilian Personnel Division, states that positions in French, German, Russian and Spanish have been filled in the last two years.

The training academies of the armed forces employ regular foreign language teachers in their foreign language departments. The head of the Foreign Language Department of the U.S. Naval

Academy in Annapolis, Maryland, states that the Academy has a staff of 46, including instructors in French, German, Italian, Portuguese, Russian, and Spanish.

At the United States Military Academy at West Point, New York, instruction is offered in Chinese, French, German, Portuguese, Russian, and Spanish. The department is staffed by regular or reserve Army officers on active duty, plus a few native-born speakers. In addition there is the Post Elementary School where a few individuals are employed in foreign language instruction.

UNITED NATIONS

The throbbing offices of the United Nations in New York, with 1,680 American employees, offer many attractive and interesting openings to trained linguists. The positions extend over a wide range, from the bilingual typist at the bottom to the highly skilled, rapid-fire interpreters at the top. The Chief of the Overseas Recruitment Section says:

> "The language posts of the United Nations Secretariat consist of translation, interpretation, verbatim reporting, summary reporting, proofreading, clerical, and secretarial. Arabic, Chinese, English, French, Russian, and Spanish are the official languages of the organization, and out of these, English and French are considered as the working languages. Hence, staff may be needed to work in the capacities enumerated above in one or more of the specified languages."

The following data are taken from a special circular issued by the United Nations entitled, *General Information on United Nations Employment Opportunities:*

The United Nations has a steady need for competent staff in various fields. While it is impossible to list in detail the different types of positions for which the organization recruits, the major categories of staff are described below. The majority of professional posts in the Secretariat are closely related to the nature of the work required by Resolutions of the General Assembly and its principal organs. As a result, the need is largely for specialized professional candidates, with a concentration in economics and related fields. Preference is given to candidates with a knowledge of both working languages of the Secretariat, i.e., English and French. In addition to professional personnel, there is a continuous need for stenographic help and linguistic staff, such as translators and interpreters, who are not subject to geographical distribution considerations.

Professional posts. The professional vacancies that occur periodically call for persons of real professional talent in fields related to the work of the United Nations. A Junior professional candidate must have an advanced university degree from a North American university, a *Licence avec mention* or a *Maitrise* from a French university, an honours degree from a British university or the equivalent from other countries. For higher level professional posts, candidates are expected to have attained, in addition to their educational background, recognized standing in their fields.

Technical Assistance experts. The United Nations Programmes of Technical Co-operation are administered by the United Nations. Personnel requests are usually for senior expert advisers, who are required to have reached the highest professional standing after long experience in their fields.

Administrative posts. Administrative vacancies are few and far between and, in any case, are normally filled by the reassignment of existing staff.

Public Information posts. Applications for appointments in the Office of Public Information are particularly numerous and, consequently, competition is keen. Preference is given to candidates able to work in more than one of the official languages.

Posts in the Office of Legal Affairs. The Office of Legal Affairs has a relatively small staff. Only candidates with specialization in public international law are considered, and preference is given to those with a working knowledge of both English and French or Spanish.

Translator/Precis-writers. Recruitment is by annual competitive examination and interview. A candidate is required to translate from at least two official languages (Arabic, Chinese, English, French, Russian, and Spanish). Translators, with the exception of those in the Arabic and Chinese Sections, are also required to serve as precis-writers.

Interpreters. Interpreters are recruited by individual examination. They are required to interpret into their mother tongue, which should be one of the six official languages of the U.N., and must have full auditory comprehension of at least two of the other official languages. Candidates may either be trained interpreters, capable of passing the qualifying examination immedi-

The United Nations Interpretation Section provides simultaneous or consecutive interpretation into Arabic, Chinese, English, French, Russian and Spanish as needed.

Photo: United Nations / M. Tsovaras.

ately, or they may be persons of suitable linguistic and general cultural background (a university degree is required) who can be trained to meet the required standard in a few weeks or months.

Librarians. Candidates for librarian posts in the Secretariat must have a degree from a recognized library school or an equivalent professional qualification and possess at least a reading knowledge of several languages, plus two or three years' professional experience.

Clerical and secretarial posts. Most vacancies are for secretaries and typists, preferably bilingual (English plus French or Spanish). Graduation from high school, or the equivalent, is required. The minimum requirements for secretarial posts are a typing speed of 50 to 60 words per minute and a stenographic speed of approximately 100 words per minute.

Guides. Guides are recruited on a local basis, usually once a year, and begin their training early in March. Only female candidates, 20 to 30 years of age, with college education or equivalent, are considered. They must be fluent in English and any other language, with a good speaking voice.

Persons who wish to be considered for employment at the U.N. should address an application to the Office of Personnel Services, United Nations, New York, N.Y. 10017.

TRANSLATOR/PRECIS-WRITER

The duties of English Translator/Precis-writer are: (a) To translate into English, for the most part from French, Russian or Spanish, but occasionally from Arabic, Chinese and other languages, documents relating to various aspects of United Nations activities, including political debates, economic, social and legal reports, international agreements, scientific and technical studies and official correspondence, and (b) To attend meetings of

United Nations bodies and draft summary records of their proceedings.

Candidates must be of English mother tongue and graduates of a university or an equivalent establishment where the language of instruction was preferably their mother tongue. "Mother tongue" is defined as the language in which the candidate has completed the essential part of her or his education and in which he or she writes correctly, with style and with a rich vocabulary reflecting a university level education.

Candidates must have a perfect command of English, a thorough knowledge of French and one other official language (Arabic, Chinese, Russian or Spanish). A knowledge of other languages is a valuable additional qualification.

The written examination, which lasts two days, consists of (1) translation into English of a French text of a general nature (3 hours), (2) translation into English of two French texts of a technical nature, chosen by the candidate from the four offered (3 hours), and (3) summary in English of a French speech (2 hours) or translation into English of a French text of a specially technical nature chosen by the candidate from the three offered.

Candidates who are successful in the written examination will be interviewed, normally seven to eight weeks after the examination, by a Board of Examiners. The interview is an integral part of the examination and candidates who are called should not assume that they will automatically be offered an appointment. The Board will recommend to the Assistant Secretary-General the most suitable candidates for appointment. Travel expenses to and from the place of interview will be reimbursed by the United Nations.

Examinations for English Translator/Precis-writer are normally held in the spring in a number of designated cities, including Geneva, London, Vienna and New York. Candidates should apply to the Office of Personnel Services, United Nations, New York, N.Y. 10017.

INTERPRETER

A special circular issued by the United Nations office entitled *Information for Persons Interested in Examinations for Interpreters* contains the following information:

• Candidates for the post of a United Nations interpreter are required to pass an examination to ascertain their professional skill and proficiency in rendering orally from one language to another speeches made at the United Nations meetings. Those considered for regular appointments (rather than temporary assistance) also are required to pass a general culture test designed to assess their educational background of world events and history, with particular emphasis on political, economic, and social questions of interest to the United Nations. Tests are arranged individually, at Headquarters in New York or at the United Nations office in Geneva, for candidates found eligible on the basis of their credentials and preliminary interview.

• United Nations interpreters must have a thorough knowledge of at least three of the Organization's official languages (Arabic, Chinese, English, French, Russian, and Spanish). As a rule, they interpret into their mother tongue and must have full auditory comprehension of at least two of the other official languages. This linguistic knowledge must cover a wide variety of fields—political, economic, legal, literary, etc. Mere ability to converse socially in several languages is not enough.

• Besides linguistic knowledge and skill, a United Nations interpreter must be a person so equipped by education and experience that he has a thorough understanding of the various subjects debated in any of the meetings to which he may be assigned—or at least the intellectual ability to acquire this understanding by study. Candidates are therefore expected to be graduates of a university or an equivalent establishment.

• Interpreters normally are offered a probationary appointment at the P-2 level. After two years of satisfactory service they are offered a permanent contract and promoted to the P-3 level, in which there are thirteen steps, each representing an annual increment. In exceptional cases appointment may be at the P-3 level. In some cases a fixed-term contract may be offered instead of a probationary appointment. Competent interpreters are eventually promoted to the P-4 level, in which there are twelve steps.

• Annual salaries for interpreters are shown in the table below. The gross salaries are subject to "staff assessment" in lieu of national income tax; net salaries are normally tax free.

In addition to the net salary, staff members receive a post adjustment varying with the cost of living at the duty station. Additional benefits not shown in the table include an annual allowance of $400 for a dependent spouse, $300 for each dependent child, education grants, installation grants, etc. Staff members are entitled to 6 weeks leave per year while in full pay status, and leave may be accumulated up to a maximum of 12 weeks. Travel costs of staff members and their families on joining the United Nations Secretariat, on home leave (every two years), and on repatriation after service are paid by the United Nations.

Annual Salary Scales as of August, 1974

	P-2		P-3		P-4	
	Minimum	Maximum	Minimum	Maximum	Minimum	Maximum
Gross	$14,780	$19,880	$18,410	$25,610	$22,680	$30,490
Net	11,346	14,722	13,766	18,366	16,542	21,294

Post Adjustment

	P-2		P-3		P-4	
Single staff members	2,016	2,592	2,424	3,180	2,892	3,600
Staff members with dependents	3,024	3,888	3,636	4,770	4,338	5,400

VERBATIM REPORTER

The following information is given with reference to the position of verbatim reporter for the U.N.

Nature of the Work

All verbatim reporting at the United Nations is what is often called "immediate copy," i.e., the transcript of a given meeting must be completed on stencils or ready for dispatch to the reproduction shop not more than 1½ hours after the end of the proceedings. This is necessitated by the rules of procedure of most United Nations bodies, which call for the distribution of the complete record to all delegations within twenty-four hours, and time must be left for the processes of reproduction, collation, and distribution of many hundreds of copies.

Consequently, the official verbatim record of a body such as the General Assembly is taken by a team of reporters numbering not less than eight (and sometimes more), who normally work on a timetable of ten-minute takes. For a meeting beginning at 3 p.m., for instance, the first reporter takes notes until 3:10, is relieved by a colleague who records from 3:10 to 3:20, and so on until all have had ten minutes of note-taking. In the meantime each, in turn, returns to the typing room and dictates to a typist, who types on stencils. Each reporter must finish dictating his first take in time to return to the meeting for a second and so on. Thus with eight reporters each has seventy minutes in which to dictate his notes and proofread the transcript of each ten-minute take. The reporter may have to record speeches made in English as well as the English interpretations of speeches made in other official languages. In this manner, most United Nations bodies have verbatim records prepared simultaneously in English, French, and Spanish.

Qualifications

A candidate for a post of verbatim reporter at the United Nations is expected to give proof of ability to take notes at not less than 200 words per minute (shorthand or stenotyping) and transcribe them accurately. Since many of the speeches are made by persons who do not speak English as their native tongue, he also is expected to be able to edit his notes as he dictates, so that at least the grosser errors of grammar and syntax are eliminated without doing violence to the meaning. Further, he must verify and correct, if necessary, all quotations included in speeches, put in references to documents, and be able to spot and correct whatever errors of fact speakers may make, or at least, recognize them as such and bring them to the attention of the chief of the service.

There are as many different accents to cope with as there are delegations, and a quick ear is essential. The reporter is also expected to be familiar in a general way with international affairs and with the history and organization of the United Nations. A knowledge of at least one of the other official languages (Arabic, French, Russian or Spanish) is very helpful. Since the material dealt with may range over many different technical subjects, the reporter can hardly have too large a vocabulary or too wide a sphere of knowledge, even if only in general terms. Finally, he must be prepared to put his whole time at the disposal of the U.N. and be ready to work at any time of the day or night, on Saturdays, and even on Sundays, often at very short notice, whenever meetings are held.

Arabic Verbatim Reporters

These reporters work in New York during the General Assembly session only. Candidates for these positions must have a few years of college education or the equivalent, with Arabic as their mother tongue. They must be able to record the minutes of meetings at a speed of not less than 140 words per minute, and it would be preferable if they had a knowledge of at least one of the other official languages.

Salary

In New York, the initial net annual salary for Verbatim Reporters (after certain deductions in lieu of national income tax) is $13,766, to which is added a net, non-pensionable post adjustment of $2,424 for a staff member with no primary dependent and $3,636 for a staff member with one primary dependent or more.

Various allowances may be added to this, according to circumstances. If one's work is satisfactory, annual increases are granted. A career reporter could, in twelve years, reach a net annual salary of $18,366, plus the various allowances mentioned above.

Terms of Appointment

Appointments are made initially for a probationary period of two years, upon the successful completion of which a permanent appointment may be awarded. A few short-term appointments are made for the duration of the General Assembly or other conferences.

SECRETARY, STENOGRAPHER, TYPIST AND CLERK

Vacancies. The only vacancies in the secretarial category open to outside applicants are at junior levels (age limits 18 to 35). Openings at senior levels are filled by promotion.

Examinations. All applicants are required to take entrance examinations held weekly at the United Nations General Recruitment Section, located at One UN Plaza, 44th Street and First Avenue, New York City. These examinations, which are given in English, French or Spanish at the choice of the candidate, are scheduled some time in advance. Interviews are conducted between 10 a.m. and 12:30 p.m., Monday to Friday, in Room DC-200. As vacancies occur, selection is made from a roster of successful candidates.

Examinations are given for clerks, typists and stenographers. *Bilingual   Secretaries,   Stenographers   and   Typists.* Languages – French/English and Spanish/English

Standards required in the candidate's best language:

Secretary and Stenographer,

90 wpm shorthand, 50 wpm typing.

Typist, 50 wpm typing.

Standards required in the candidate's second language:

Secretary and Stenographer,

80 wpm shorthand, 50 wpm typing.

Typist, 50 wpm typing.

Technical qualifications of candidates are tested in group examinations. Candidates may also be asked to draft a short letter in both languages.

Education. Graduation from a high school or equivalent. Background and work experience determine the starting salary.

Medical Examination. All appointments are subject to the successful passing of the medical examination, normally given at United Nations Headquarters.

Salary. According to background and experience, the gross annual salaries range from $14,300 to $38,190, ($11,917 to $26,298 net after the deduction of "Staff Assessment" which is a system of internal taxation applicable to United Nations employees). In addition, certain allowances and benefits, such as pension fund, medical insurance, sick leave, etc., are available under the United Nations Staff Regulations and Staff Rules. Annual leave accrues at the rate of 2½ days a month, or 30 working days a year.

Opportunities for Advancement. The scale of salaries comprises five grade levels with 9 to 10 steps in each grade. Annual within-grade increments are given on the basis of satisfactory service. Promotions are based on merit and length of service. At the present time, salaries in the General Service Category go as high as $23,910, or $17,341 net per annum.

Overseas Mission Assignment. A staff member with a permanent appointment (normally granted after 2 years of service) who has reached the age of 24, may apply for a mission assignment. The United Nations has field missions in many parts of the world.

Language Instruction. Free language courses in the six official languages (Arabic, Chinese, English, French, Russian and Spanish) are available and staff members are encouraged to enroll in them. Successful completion of the course entitles the staff member to a language allowance of $506 net per annum. In cases where a staff member is proficient in two of the official languages, another $253 net per annum is given for proficiency in a third language.

UNITED NATIONS GUIDES

In addition to the positions at the United Nations for which fluency in a foreign language is the major requirement, there are a number of other jobs in which such ability is not absolutely necessary but is helpful. One of the most interesting of these, open only to women between the ages of 20 and 30, is that of guiding visitors through the United Nations Headquarters.

Guides are expected to conduct five and possibly six tours a day. They work five days a week, including Saturdays and Sundays. In addition, there are some half-time guides, who work twenty hours a week, again including weekends.

The initial salary is $773 gross ($621 net) monthly. Half-time guides earn one-half of this amount. Initial appointment is for a probationary period of three months. There is a short paid training period. Annual leave is 30 working days a year.

Candidates must be fluent in English, with a good speaking voice. Fluency in other languages is desirable. Applicants must be in excellent physical condition and of attractive appearance.

Guides are recruited on a local basis once a year and begin their training during the early part of March. A personal interview at Headquarters is required, and the most convenient time for this is from October through December. For the recruitment of candidates, the United Nations does not use commercial employment agencies. Qualified candidates are, therefore, invited to apply directly to their New York offices.

PEACE CORPS

The Peace Corps is an extremely interesting opportunity for young people who are ready to serve as volunteers in the improvement of international relations and who are eager to live in a foreign country.

Founded in 1961, the Peace Corps became a part of ACTION in 1971, when ACTION was formed to bring together all citizen volunteer programs administered by the federal government.

Peace Corps volunteers share their skills and train people in developing nations around the world. In many instances, Peace Corps volunteers are the only Americans living and working as a part of local communities in these countries. They gain credibility and prove effective because they speak the language of the people, appreciate local customs, and adapt to living and working conditions, which are often considerably different from those at home.

Peace Corps volunteers strive to create mutual understanding between Americans and the people with whom they are living and working. More than 6,000 volunteers serve today in more than sixty countries. Their experience is in general a satisfying one; in a survey of volunteers, 92 percent said they would gladly serve again. Since 1961 the Peace Corps has sent more than 72,000 volunteers abroad.

An interpreter aids Secretary General Kurt Waldheim and Mrs. Edward Gierek, wife of the First Secretary of the Central Committee, Poland, in conversation at a United Nations state dinner.

Peace Corps volunteers must be U.S. citizens, 18 years or over, in good health, and willing to serve abroad for at least two years. Every applicant must submit to a medical examination. Although competence in a foreign language is not an absolute requirement it is, of course, a great asset. French is particularly desirable. Essential are a college degree and skill in one of the more than 300 categories. These include accountancy, agriculture, architecture, medicine, horticulture, therapy, plumbing, nursing, education, etc.

Training is provided for the two-year assignment. Medical care and transportation are taken care of. The monthly subsistence allowance covers food, lodging and incidentals. There is no salary. At the end of the service the volunteer receives an adjustment allowance of $125 for every month served, including the training period. Two months vacation are granted.

In the foreign country, the volunteers work for a government department or agency, under the supervision of local officials. They speak the language of the people and are subject to local laws.

One very important area is teaching. Assignments are as varied as the cultures in which they operate. Some volunteers teach in major cities; others in rural areas. Volunteers are needed for almost every field of education—elementary, secondary and college teaching; commercial, health, special education.

Application may be made at any of the ACTION Recruitment Regional Offices which are found in most of the major cities of the country. The Peace Corps service is so many-sided and fascinating, that one may say that it is not just a preparation for a career, but a preparation for life.

INTERNATIONAL STUDENT INFORMATION SERVICE

The International Student Information Service maintains an office at 133 Rue Hotel des Monnaies, Brussels 6, Belgium. The

International Student Travel Center, an affiliate of ISIS, is at 866 United Nations Plaza, New York, New York 10017.

The ISIS places teachers and students in overseas positions. Opportunities for Americans with only one language other than English are few. Non-teaching jobs are available to persons between 17 and 40 years of age, who wish to earn their living expenses during a two-month summer stay abroad. If they stay longer, they may be able to earn more. The multilingual student has considerable opportunity for placement even in distant countries of the world.

The available jobs range from baby-sitters, hotel receptionists, waiters and waitresses to office workers and camp counselors. The countries to be visited are divided into four language areas: English, (Great Britain and Denmark); German, (Switzerland, Austria and West Germany), and other (Spain, Portugal, Italy, Japan, Africa). Students who are interested should write to the ISIS office in Brussels.

CHAPTER 7

TEACHING

Teaching is one of the largest of the professions. There are about three million men and women serving as teachers in the various educational establishments of the country—elementary and secondary schools, private and parochial schools, colleges and universities. In addition, there are thousands of persons who teach part-time.

Of this large staff, about 80,000 are teachers of foreign languages. Some 50,000 are in junior and senior high schools and 25,000 in colleges and universities. Besides these, there are several thousand foreign language teachers in elementary schools, not to mention private and parochial schools. There are also many commercial schools teaching foreign languages; there are 31 of these in New York City alone.

Corresponding to the enrollments in the various languages, the number of teachers in descending order are in Spanish, French, German, Latin, Russian, Italian, Chinese, Greek, and Japanese. Two new educational programs must be included in the foreign language picture, namely, Bilingual Education and TESOL—teaching English as a second language.

Because of the tightening of the educational situation and because of the lowering of language requirements for admission and degrees, competition for language teaching jobs has become keen. School boards now usually require a bachelor's degree, with competency in two languages or in a language and another subject. It is of great advantage to the applicant if he can offer experience in practice teaching, a state certificate, and travel or study in the foreign country in addition to his other qualifications. In view of present conditions, it is highly advisable for every language teacher to acquire some fluency in Spanish.

Despite the decline in foreign language enrollments during the last few years, there are a number of factors which present favorable prospects for the young college graduate. If he or she is ready to accept a starting salary lower than that of the older, more experienced teacher and is agreeable to a position in a smaller or rural community, the likelihood of being placed is not too dim. Although the public schools in general pay much better, the atmosphere and the working conditions in many private and parochial schools are more attractive and may make up for the lower pay.

As in other fields, there has been a marked increase in teachers' salaries in recent years. In 1978 the median salary for secondary school teachers was $15,000. In New York City the maximum salary of a high school teacher is now over $25,000.

As has been pointed out before, the foreign language teaching area has become somewhat restricted within recent years. Two adjacent fields, however, have opened up, which give great promise of considerably increased enrollments and many more jobs for teachers. These are Bilingual Education and TESOL.

BILINGUAL EDUCATION

The rapid proliferation of bilingual education throughout the country is something startlingly new in school practices. It has expanded widely since the federal government passed the Bilingual Education Act in 1967. It allotted millions of dollars for the financing of programs to help pupils with a limited knowledge of English. The total federal grant for 1979-80 amounted to $94,557,731.

This is a recent development. Only a few years ago not a single state required bilingual teaching and twenty-two forbade it by law. Today more than a dozen states demand some form of bilingual instruction. The Department of Health, Education and Welfare sponsors 627 bilingual projects in 68 languages. These programs include teacher training, curriculum development and classroom techniques.

Almost five million children are involved. A recent tabulation:

Mexican American	3,100,000
Puerto Rican	800,000
Other Spanish	380,000
French speaking	350,000
American Indian & Eskimo	180,000
Portuguese	60,000
Chinese	40,000
Japanese	20,000
Russian	8,000
Chamarro	7,500
Other	10,000
	4,955,500

Bilingual teachers are expected to speak English and a second language fluently and to be acquainted with both cultures. They should also be thoroughly grounded in the elementary school curriculum or a major high school subject—science, mathematics, social studies, etc. Because of these new requirements, schools of education and teachers colleges have hastened to set up special training courses.

The U.S. Office of Bilingual Education maintains a teacher training program, for which a fund of more than $11 million has been allotted. There are 103 projects in which 4,423 trainees are involved in 27 states. Some 25 languages are taught.

In the Regional Bilingual Training Resource Center in New York, the following languages are represented: Arabic, Chinese, French, Greek, Haitian, Italian, Korean, Spanish and Yiddish. Over 300,000 pupils are participating in the program.

ESL

The ESL program involves the teaching of English as a second language. ESL teachers must complete a specific training program that includes comparative linguistics to be certified to teach ESL in public schools. The ESL program has been very successful, and is also in use in Australia, New Zealand, South Africa, and a number of Latin-American countries, including Mexico, Colombia and Venezuela.

Programs like ESL, FLES, and bilingual programs have reached many thousands of students in the United States and other countries.

Other organizations such as the YMCA and local chambers of commerce sometimes offer classes in English to speakers of other languages. A number of commercial language schools specialize in teaching English to speakers of other languages.

FLES

The teaching of Foreign Languages in the Elementary Schools goes back to the middle of the 19th century when French and German were widely taught in the grades. It continued after the turn of the century until the outbreak of World War I.

FLES became a nation-wide educational phenomenon after May 2, 1952 when Earl J. McGrath, U.S. Commissioner of Education, vigorously stressed the importance of foreign language study. There was an almost immediate response and FLES programs were established throughout the country.

The leading languages were French, German, Italian, Russian and Spanish. Extensive FLES programs flourished in Chicago, Cleveland, Detroit and St. Louis. In New York French and Spanish were introduced as part of an enrichment program for intellectually gifted children. At present FLES is linked in many schools with the bilingual education program.

COLLEGE TEACHING

With the dropping of foreign language requirements for college admission and college degrees, a drastic decline in language enrollments set in. That, of course, meant fewer positions for instructors. The requirements for the job, however, were not lowered. Professors at four-year colleges are usually expected to have completed doctoral programs and are expected to continue scholarly research and publishing throughout their careers.

Graduate students, especially at large universities, can support themselves and gain experience by teaching undergraduate language courses as teaching assistants, or TAs. In some instances instructors without bachelor's degrees are hired if they can teach a rare language for which there are few qualified teachers. For this sort of job, native speakers are given the preference. Positions are usually part-time and the pay is not high.

At two-year colleges some states require instructors to hold teaching certificates. In general, a master's degree is required. The teaching load is frequently heavier at four-year colleges. The demand for research and publishing are less stringent, and, generally, salaries are lower.

Private commercial language schools and federal language schools usually hire native speakers as teachers. The positions are frequently part-time. In the bigger cities there are a considerable number of language schools. In New York, for instance, there are more than forty.

THE PRESIDENT'S COMMISSION ON FOREIGN LANGUAGES

During the last few years the outlook for study of foreign languages in the United States has not been very bright. Enrollments dropped drastically, largely because colleges and universities dropped the foreign language requirement for admission and for degrees. The situation became so alarming that it was pointed out to President Carter, and he appointed a Commission of Foreign Languages and International Studies. The Commission set to work and in October of 1979 submitted a report to the President, presenting a long list of recommendations.

A few of those that relate directly or indirectly to job opportunities are the following:

The U.S. Department of Education should establish 20 regional centers to study and upgrade foreign language teaching at all levels.

From 20-30 summer institutes should be offered abroad annually.

Colleges and universities should reinstate foreign language requirements.

The Department of Education should provide incentive funding to schools for foreign language teaching.

The Secretary of Education should declare foreign languages a top priority and encourage their increased support from kindergarten through twelfth grade.

The Department of Education should fund 200 undergraduate international studies programs at a total cost of $8 million a year.

The program envisioned by the Commission is of vast scope and dimensions. Its success will depend largely upon the funds allotted for its realization. In any case, public attention has been focused on the importance of foreign language studies and it is quite certain that this area will acquire new life. If only a portion of the recommendations are carried out, it should result in a considerable increase in student enrollments. This, of course, will mean more jobs for teachers.

RECOMMENDED READING

The works listed below are not intended as a complete or scholarly compilation of books on foreign language study. They are merely a listing of some of the more recent and practical publications which may be of help to a student planning a foreign language career.

FOREIGN SERVICE

Best Opportunities for Federal Employment. U.S. Civil Service Commission, Washington, D.C. 20415.

Examination for Foreign Service Officer Careers. Department of State Publication, Superintendent of Documents, U.S. Government Printing Office, Washington, D.C. 20401.

1973 Examinations for Foreign Service Officer Careers. Department of State Publication. Available from: Board of Examiners for the Foreign Service, Box 9317 Rosslyn Station, Arlington, Va. 22209.

Career in Foreign Service of the United States. State Department Publication 7924. Washington, D.C. 20520.

Occupational Outlook Reprint Series. 152 bulletins. Available from the Superintendent of Documents, U.S. Government Printing Office, Washington, D.C. 20401, or from any of the regional offices of the Bureau of Labor Statistics.

Occupational Outlook Handbook. U.S. Department of Labor. U.S. Government Printing Office, Washington, D.C. 20401.

Careers in Cross-Cultural Communication. U.S. Information Agency. Washington, D.C. 20521.

Foreign Service of the Seventies. Department of State Publication 8535, Department and Foreign Service Series 142. U.S. Government Printing Office, Washington, D.C. 20401.

Diplomacy for the 70's. Department of State Publication 8551, Department and Foreign Service Series 143. U.S. Government Printing Office, Washington, D.C. 20401.

The Information Machine: The USIA And American Foreign Policy. Robert Elder. Syracuse, University of Syracuse Press.

The United States Information Agency. John W. Henderson. New York: Praeger Publishing.

Cultural Affairs and Foreign Policy. American Assembly. Braisted, Paul J., Ed. Washington, D.C.: Columbia Books.

Public Diplomacy and the Behavioral Sciences. Glen H. Fisher. Bloomington: Indiana University Press.

The Foreign Service of the United States. William Barnes and John Heath-Morgan. New York: Praeger Publishing.

Fires in the In-Basket. John Leacocos. New York: World.

The Professional Diplomat. John E. Harr. Princeton: Princeton University Press.

The Neglected Aspect of Foreign Affairs: American Educational and Cultural Policy Abroad. Charles Frankel. Washington, D.C.: The Brookings Institution.

Opportunities in Foreign Service Careers. Lucile Harrigan. Louisville, Ky.: Vocational Guidance Manuals.

EXPORT TRADE

So You Want An Assignment Overseas. Alex J. Wertis. New York: U.S. Steel Export Co.

Export Trade. Published every Monday by Thomas Ashwell & Co., 20 Vessey St., New York, N.Y.

Publications of the Latin American Institute, 292 Madison Ave.,
New York, N.Y. Also, *The Bilingual Secretary; Educational
Opportunities; Careers in Languages.*

TEACHING LANGUAGES

Overseas. The Magazine of Educational Exchange, published by
the Institute of International Education, 800 Second Ave.,
New York, N.Y. 10017.

Why Johnny Should Learn Foreign Languages. Theodore Huebener. Philadelphia: Chilton Co.

A Handbook of Bilingual Education. Muriel R. Saville and Ru-
dolph C. Troike. Teachers of English to Speakers of Other
Languages. Washington, D.C.

Bilingual Review. Published by Board of Education of New York
City, 110 Livingston St., Brooklyn, N.Y. 11201. Published
bi-monthly.

ADFL. Bulletin of the Association of Departments of Foreign
Languages. Published four times a year. MLA, 62 Fifth Ave.,
New York 10011.

CAREERS

Career Opportunities as a Foreign Service Officer. Department
of State Publications: 7245. U.S. Government Printing
Office, Washington, D.C.

Foreign Languages and Your Career. U.S. Department of Labor,
Washington, D.C. Free publication.

Foreign Languages and Careers. Lucille Honig and Richard I.
Brod. *Modern Language Journal,* April 1974. pp. 157-185.
Reprint Mod.Lang. Assn.

Bibliography and Materials on Foreign Languages and Careers.
Barbara Elling, State University of New York, Stony Brook,
N.Y., 1978.

LANGUAGE ASSOCIATIONS AND JOURNALS

Modern Language Association of
  America (MLA)
62 Fifth Avenue
New York, N.Y. 10011

National Federation of Modern
  Language Teachers Associations
212 Crosby Hall
State Univ. of New York at Buffalo
Buffalo, New York 14214

Publishes the *Modern
Language Journal* eight
times a year.

American Council on the
  Teaching of Foreign Languages
2 Park Avenue
New York, N.Y. 10016

Publishes the ACTFL
  *Foreign Language
  Education Series.*

L'Alliance Francaise &
  French Institute
22 E. 60th Street
New York, N.Y. 10023

Hispanic Society of America
Broadway Between 155th &
  156th Streets
New York, N.Y. 10032

Societe des Professeurs de
  Francais en Amerique
3 E. 95th Street
New York, N.Y. 10025

Goethe House
1014 Fifth Avenue
New York, N.Y. 10028

French Embassy
Cultural Division
927 Fifth Avenue
New York, N.Y. 10028

Organization of American States
17th and Constitution Ave.
Washington, D.C. 20001

National Hebrew Culture Council
1776 Broadway
New York, N.Y. 10019

VIVO Institute for Jewish
  Research
1048 Fifth Avenue
New York, N.Y. 10028

Leo Baeck Institute
129 E. 73rd Street
New York, N.Y. 10023

American Association of
  Teachers of French
57 East Armory Avenue
Champaign, Illinois 61820

Publishes the *French
Review* six times a year.

American Association of
  Teachers of German
523 Building, Route 38
Cherry Hill, N.J. 08034

Publishes the *German
Quarterly* five times a year.

American Association of
  Teachers of Italian
Rutgers University
New Brunswick, N.J. 08903

Publishes *Italica* four times
a year.

American Association of Teachers
  of Spanish and Portuguese
Wichita State University
Wichita, Kansas 67208

Publishes *Hispania* four
times a year.

GOVERNMENT OFFICES

U.S. Department of State
Employment Division
Washington, D.C. 20520

Board of Examiners for the
 Foreign Service
Box 9317 - Rosslyn Station,
Arlington, Virginia 22209

Recruitment and Examining
 Division
United States Information
 Agency
1776 Pennsylvania Ave., N.W.
Washington, D.C. 20547

U.S. Information Agency
Office of Personnel and
 Training
1776 Pennsylvania Ave., N.W.
Washington, D.C. 20547

Department of Commerce
Bureau of International Commerce
Washington, D.C. 20230

Agency for International
 Development
Recruitment, Office of Personnel
419 Pomponio Plaza,
Washington, D.C. 20523

Central Intelligence Agency
P.O. Box 9312
Rosslyn Station,
Arlington, Virginia 22209

Defense Intelligence Agency
 Civilian Personnel Branch
Recruitment Section
The Pentagon
Washington, D.C. 20301

U.S. Civil Service Commission
1900 E Street, N.W.
Washington, D.C. 20415

Office of Information and
  Publications

Bureau of Customs
  Department of Treasury
Washington, D.C. 20226

Immigration and Naturalization Service
Department of Justice
119 D Street, N.E.
Washington, D.C. 20536

Director of Personnel
United Nations Headquarters
1 United Nations Plaza
New York, N.Y. 10017

Manpower Administration
U.S. Department of Labor
Washington, D.C. 20210

Director of Recruitment
Peace Corps
806 Connecticut Ave., N.W.
Washington, D.C. 20202